# LEON
# *Fast*
# Vegetarian

JANE BAXTER &
HENRY DIMBLEBY

PHOTOGRAPHY BY GEORGIA GLYNN SMITH · DESIGN BY ANITA MANGAN

conran
OCTOPUS

To my wife, Jemima. This is the third Leon book that she has worked on tirelessly. Reading draft after draft. Editing my abysmal grammar. Adding some good jokes. And being endlessly supportive. Also to our children George, Johnny and Dory for putting up with my culinary adventures with such apparent enthusiasm.
HENRY

To my son David … who is, without a doubt, the best travel companion anyone could wish for and apparently a 'double adventurer' too.
JANE

# Contents

**PART ONE** STAR TURNS: Dishes that can stand alone as a whole meal **24**

**PART TWO** SUPPORTING CAST: Grazing dishes, sides, relishes & puddings **194**

# Welcome to Leon Fast Vegetarian

This book was conceived in the back of a bus in Italy. We were on a cooking, or more strictly eating, tour of Alba. In the gaps between gastronomic blow-outs we started musing on the need for a book that would help people make the most of their vegetables without spending hours in the kitchen.

People often go one of two ways with vegetables. They either try to make them more approachable – more meat-like – by slathering them with sauces, shaping them into burgers and shrouding them in pastry; or they turn to the exotic, relying on specialist ingredients and fistfuls of pomegranate seeds.

Although both approaches can yield treasures, we wanted to strip things back a little: let the vegetables themselves stand out. You will find flavours in this book from all over the world – we are both keen travellers – but the recipes have deliberately been kept simple, with ingredients that are easily available from markets, allotments, veg boxes and supermarkets. We hope that experienced and nervous cooks alike will find plenty of inspiration.

The book is divided into two parts. The first, Star Turns, is a collection of dishes that can stand alone as a whole meal, with ideas for breakfast, pasta, grains, pulses, pies and bakes, and curries. The second part, Supporting Cast, is full of side dishes and smaller plates. Things you could put together to create a meal or (whisper it) which might go well alongside a central meat dish.

As with any Leon book, it's not about spending hours in the kitchen but about bringing family and friends together with simple, gutsy, happy-making food.

Henry & Jane

THE DIMBLEBY FAMILY, 1976

## KEY TO SYMBOLS

| | |
|---|---|
| W F | Wheat Free |
| G F | Gluten Free |
| D F | Dairy Free |
| V | Vegetarian |
| ♥ | Low Saturated Fats |
| ✓ | Low GL |
| 🍴 | Indulgence |
| TIPS | Recipe tips and serving suggestions |
| VARIATIONS | Ideas for alternative ingredients |

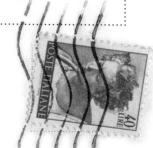

# A note about Jane by Henry

I first met Jane in the Riverford Farm field kitchen, where she was formerly head chef.

It calls itself a field kitchen because it is, pretty much, a kitchen in a field. Or more truthfully, a smart wooden barn, looking out on to rows of sweetcorn, pumpkins or whatever crops are coming into season.

The lunch that followed changed the way I thought about vegetables. There is one service, with no choice. Guests all sit together hugger-mugger at long trestle tables, and serve themselves from huge platters – usually five or six different vegetable dishes and only one of meat.

I had never before eaten vegetables that felt so much like the stars of the show. The meat seemed like no more than a garnish: a decorative frippery beside the jewel-like mounds of succulent veg. I asked to meet the chef who had wrought such miracles, and was introduced to Jane.

Since then, we have become friends, and Jane has changed the way I cook. She is my 'phone a friend' when I am staring at my veg box and lacking in inspiration. She is probably the greatest vegetable cook in Britain – and much more besides. She is just as handy with meat, and most importantly, she is a wonderful friend – smiling, funny and teasing.

As I left the farm after that first lunch, Jane encouraged me to pull one of the ripening sweetcorn cobs straight off the stem and take a bite. It was as sweet as a peach, and totally surprising. Just like her.

# A note about Henry

Henry founded Leon restaurants in 2004 with John Vincent. They had a shared vision: to make it easy for everyone to eat good food.

Henry started his career as a commis chef with the Michelin-starred chef Bruno Loubet, but discovered he lacked the dexterity to make ornamental carrots. So instead he became a journalist, and later a management consultant.

It was then that he met John. While working together they travelled all over the country. All they found to eat on their trips was delicious but life-destroying fried chicken or cold neon-lit sandwiches. Infuriated by the difficulty of finding tasty, nutritious food on the run, they resolved to do something about it themselves. And so Leon was born.

# From Garden to Plate

BY TOM MOGGACH

TOM MOGGACH, 1979

## SEEDS

I met Tom when he answered a tweeted plea for scaffolding planks (they make excellent shelves when sanded gently and painted with a high gloss varnish). He had seen some planks lurking at the bottom of his allotment and brokered a deal for me. When I picked them up we got talking about growing vegetables to eat from small plots. As well as being a writer, Tom helps schools set up and run kitchen gardens and outdoor classrooms. He was full of brilliant practical advice, much of which he has kindly shared here. If you are hungry for more, his book *The Urban Kitchen Gardener* is a treasure trove. Check out his website too at www.cityleaf.co.uk

HENRY

If you love to cook, the natural next step is to grow your own ingredients. Not all of them, of course – just a killer shortlist of plants to add magic in the kitchen.

So what should you choose? If you struggle for time and space, it definitely pays to be ruthless. Focus on plants that (a) are easy to grow; (b) are fantastic ingredients; (c) crop heavily; (d) are expensive or hard to buy in the shops.

Don't bother with the dull staples. Onions, for example, cost pennies to buy in the shops, so what's the point?

I've suggested my favourite food plants (see page 10) and offered some tips for making the most of any plot, from a window ledge to a back garden.

But first, a few lessons I've learnt. As you garden, experiment with how you harvest your plants – this is when you start to unlock their creative potential in the kitchen.

Try eating different parts of the plant, or sample them at different stages in their life cycles. Take coriander, for example. We're all familiar with this herb's leaves. But the flowers are also a delight, and the spicy green seeds are even better. With radishes, you can eat the root, leaves, flowers and seedpods. The list goes on …

Picking plants young offers further benefits. Baby carrots and micro herbs, for example, are gourmet ingredients and fetch a hefty price tag with chefs. But if you grow them yourself, you can choose exactly when to put them on the plate.

## YOUR PLOT

### Veg on the ledge: Window sills & ledges

There's a big difference between plants grown indoors and those grown outside. Indoor windowsills with decent light offer a cosy, sheltered environment – ideal for raising seedlings prior to life in the big outdoors. But if you're sowing seeds, be careful if there's a radiator beneath or nearby, as jolts in temperature can cause erratic germination. Better to start them off elsewhere.

With all indoor plants, remember that they soak up light from just one direction, through the glass. This can make them grow wonky. So give pots or seed trays a turn every few days.

With outdoor window ledges, choose the largest window boxes or containers that will comfortably fit. Perhaps you can further expand capacity: coax climbing plants, such as beans, up the sides; let trailing plants dangle off the edges; install extra brackets to create further levels for growing. Ensure all pots and troughs are safely secured.

### Balconies

Create different tiers or levels to boost your space. Add shelving, or make or buy a 'ladder allotment', positioning plants on the different steps. High-rise balconies can be windy – if that's the case, add windbreaks such as netting or trellis and opt for compact or dwarf varieties of plants.

### Patios

The sunniest walls are your prime spot for vertical growing. You could even paint them white to bounce the light. Use trellis or something similar to support plants. Trained fruit trees, such as espalier apples, can hug the walls. If the patio is paved, grow your plants in pots and containers or build raised beds. Or consider prising up paving slabs and creating growing zones, improving the soil where necessary.

### Roofs

Be realistic – access and water are key issues. It's no fun lugging water up flights of stairs. Ideally, install a tap. Weight is the other consideration, so commission a survey from a structural engineer if you're building a garden from scratch.

Obviously, rooftops are exposed to the elements. So while the site might be a blissful suntrap on a sunny day, poor weather and strong winds in winter can wreak havoc – make your plans with the worst in mind.

### Gardens

Sketch a plan for your vegetable garden. Herbs and salads, for example, are best within easy reach of the kitchen door. In general, long-lived plants are best off growing in the soil; use pots and containers for fast-growing annuals.

If cats, squirrels or birds are a pesky problem, rebuff them by adding a netted frame around your vegetable beds.

Neat and tidy gardens are no help to wildlife – allow a couple of tucked-away spots to grow messy.

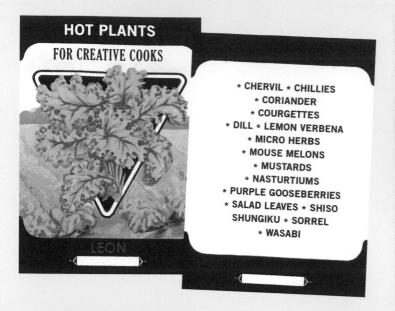

## HOT PLANTS
### FOR CREATIVE COOKS

* CHERVIL * CHILLIES
* CORIANDER
* COURGETTES
* DILL * LEMON VERBENA
* MICRO HERBS
* MOUSE MELONS
* MUSTARDS
* NASTURTIUMS
* PURPLE GOOSEBERRIES
* SALAD LEAVES * SHISO
SHUNGIKU * SORREL
* WASABI

LEON

## TO GROW MICRO HERBS:

Fill a shallow seed tray with compost, water it until moist but not wet, then sow thickly with herb seed. Cover with a plastic bag or similar while the seeds are germinating, checking on their progress each day. Remove the cover as soon as they sprout, and grow on in steady light. Then harvest the micro herbs with scissors. This technique works well with basil, chervil, coriander, dill, fennel, rocket, sorrel and many others.

*Search for the following companies online:*

### SEED SUPPLIERS:

**CN Seeds**, for unusual Oriental varieties.
**Edwin Tucker**, leading organic supplier.
**Evergreen Seeds**, Californian supplier of more than 350 Asian vegetable varieties.
**Heritage Seed Library**, a membership scheme offering access to forgotten seed varieties.
**Thomas Etty**, supplier of heritage seeds and bulbs.
**Real Seeds**, for open-pollinated and offbeat varieties.
**Jungle Seeds**, suppliers of less familiar plants such as mouse melons.

### PLANT NURSERIES:

**Blackmoor**, for fruit of all kinds.
**Edulis**, for unusual edibles.
**Organic Plants**, for 'plug' or baby plants.
**Poyntzfield Herb Nursery**, for a wide range of herbs.
**Sea Spring Seeds**, for chilli plants.

# Gardening With Children

BY TOM MOGGACH

Children can be infuriating. We love them, of course, but their fussy eating habits, wilful ways and gnat-sized attention spans can drive every parent to distraction.

Gardening can work wonders as a brilliant way of getting children outdoors and engaged. Growing their own food will also transform their eating habits and their attitude to fruit and veg.

Children will try absolutely anything if they've grown it themselves. I've watched school children I work with grazing like lambs on spicy mustard leaves, much to the amazement of their parents.

On a deeper note, learning to grow food and feed ourselves is also a fundamental life skill. So starting children off young is the right thing to do, and nurtures a sense of responsibility.

But let's be realistic. As adults, we often garden to relax – yet adding children to the mix can be stressful. I started off having naïve visions of simple days spent on the plot with my daughter, with her weeding contentedly as I toiled in the soil. But the first time we tried she pulled up my seedlings, got frustrated and threw a strop – and we beat a hasty retreat. So here are some top ideas for keeping your children keen and interested.

## THE PLOT

Let your child have a patch of soil or a collection of pots they can call their own. If possible, place it in your line of sight so that you can keep an eye on them when you're gardening or in the kitchen.

If you have the space, devote an area solely to digging. It's amazing how much children love it, and it helps to tire them out.

Mess is good. Discard adult preconceptions about how their plot should look. Children don't rate a neat lawn or tidy border, and may prefer the weeds to the cultivated plants.

## THE PLANTS

Fire up the senses: choose plants to nibble, sniff and stroke. A mini herb patch, for example, can be a multi-sensory marvel, and handling plants helps children learn how to be gentle. Lemon verbena is one of my favourite herbs, with a fabulous scent reminiscent of lemon drops. Mint is another winner, and always reminds children of toothpaste.

Prioritize plants that grow quickly. Squashes and courgettes, for example, go like the clappers. Beans are always fun and are useful for growing vertically in a compact space. Spuds are dead easy and can be grown in sacks or containers – digging up the harvest is an unforgettable buzz. Carrots are slower, but the pleasure of tugging them out of the soil never wanes.

Edible flowers bring valuable colour to the plot. Nasturtiums are my all-time favourite, as they thrive on neglect. Children, like bees, are drawn to their colour.

**Top edible plants for children:** beans, blueberries, carrots, courgettes, herbs, mouse melons, mustards, nasturtiums, peas, potatoes, radishes, salads, squashes, strawberries, tomatoes.

## THE HARVEST

Eat, eat, eat – get children in the habit of grazing on the plot. This helps to cement the vital connection between growing and eating, raising awareness of where food comes from.

Saving seeds is fun and easy. Make a point of letting a few plants go to seed to illustrate the life cycle of plants. Children love collecting seeds and writing the labels. Nasturtiums, peas and beans are among the easiest to try.

## THE NITTY GRITTY

Watering can be a minefield. Children often drown plants with enthusiasm. A nifty bit of kit is the bottle-top waterer – essentially a fine rose that you screw on to an empty water bottle. These are easy to use and provide a delicate spray that won't damage plants. Another trick is to give children a reference point for how much water is needed. 'Soak the tomatoes until you count up to twenty,' for example.

If you're sowing seeds, avoid handing children the open packet – you may end up with a trillion lettuces. Give children roughly the correct number and encourage them to position the seeds on top of the compost first. Check they have done it right before they push them in with their fingers. Show them the picture on the packet so they can see what they're aiming for.

## THE CREEPY CRAWLIES

Worms and other creatures are a source of endless fascination. Invest in a wormery, their own 'worm farm'. These composting devices are both children-friendly and a brilliant way to recycle food waste. Establish a routine of feeding them, like you would with any pet.

# PROJECTS

## MINI GARDENS

Perfect for a rainy afternoon, these miniature creations are far funkier than a dolls' house. I've seen large terracotta pots stuffed with cacti and arranged with figurines of cowboys and Indians – a Wild West masterpiece.

To get you going, other ideas include leopard-print deckchairs from material scraps, beanpoles from cocktail sticks, greenhouses from water bottles and ponds from mirrors or foil. Patches of real compost can also be sprinkled with seeds, to stunning effect.

A bowl, tray, shallow box, seed tray or trug are ideal for the base; plasticine or similar can be used for details such as tiny carrots.

## FRUIT AND VEGETABLE CREATURES

These don't require much explanation – just oodles of imagination. Broad beans make fine legs and arms, for example; blueberries become excellent eyes; cabbage leaves can be trimmed into wings. Upturned flowers make splendid hats. Use cocktail sticks to pin the fruit and vegetables together.

DAISY WITH HER VEGETABLE CREATURE

CHILDREN IN THE OUTDOOR CLASSROOM AT RHYL PRIMARY SCHOOL, LONDON

LIZA & HENRY, 1977

# Jane's Larder

These are the basic ingredients that I keep in my larder to add to vegetable dishes. It's a longish list, but a good one.

## FLOURS

Plain
Self-raising
Gram flour
Rice flour
'00' flour
Bicarbonate of soda
Baking powder

## SUGARS

Honey
Maple syrup
Soft brown sugar

## NUTS

Pine nuts
Pistachios
Walnuts
Pecans
Ground and
    flaked almonds
Peanuts
Hazelnuts

## ITALIAN

Tomato purée
Tinned chopped
    tomatoes
Dried porcini
Peeled red
    peppers
Capers (salted if
    possible)
Olives

## GRAINS & PASTA

Penne
Orecchiette
Arborio rice
Polenta
Basmati rice
Farro
Pearl barley
Couscous

## OILS

Very good-quality
    extra virgin olive
    oil for dressings
Basic extra virgin
    olive oil for cooking
Sesame oil
Walnut/hazelnut oil

## HERBS & SPICES

Ground and stick
    cinnamon
Cumin seeds
Turmeric
Curry leaves
Black mustard seeds
Cardamom
Garam masala
Szechuan peppercorns
Caraway seeds
Fennel seeds
Smoked and sweet
    paprika
Saffron
Sesame seeds
Dried thyme

## PULSES

Haricot/cannellini beans
Chickpeas
Puy (or Castelluccio) lentils
Fava beans
Black beans
Red lentils
*Dried beans are more economical, but use tinned for speed if no pre-cooked dried beans are available.*

## ASIAN

Desiccated
    coconut
Soy sauce
Kecap manis
Coconut milk
Miso paste

## VINEGARS

Rice vinegar
Balsamic vinegar
Red and white
    wine vinegar
    (or cider vinegar)

## OTHER

Pumpkin seed oil
Panko
    breadcrumbs
Squeezy Marmite
Truffle oil
Tahini
Raisins/sultanas
Mustard

## IN THE FRIDGE

Tofu and
    tempeh
Various
    cheeses
    and butter

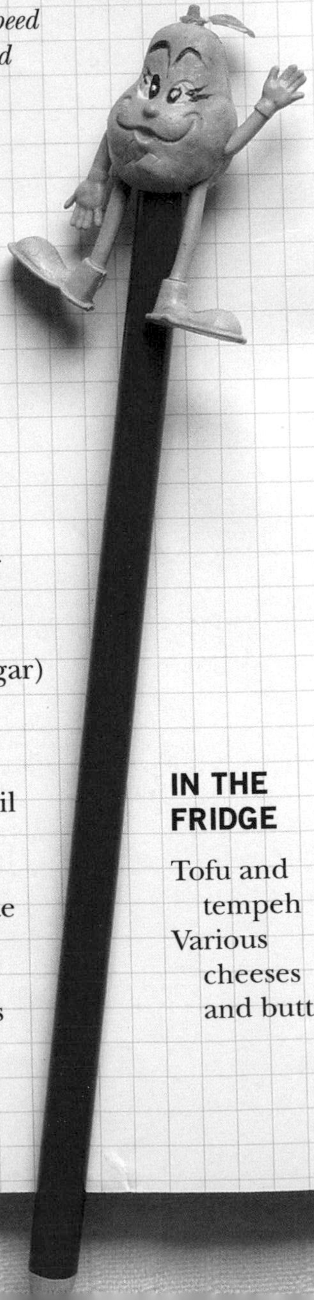

# Happy Families

There are many recipes in this book that would work just as well if you substituted the main ingredient for something similar. To help you create great dishes with whatever you have available, rather than slavishly shopping for specific vegetables, we've put together this simple guide to vegetable families.

## GREEN BEANS

Broad beans • French and runner beans • Peas • Mangetout • Sugar snaps

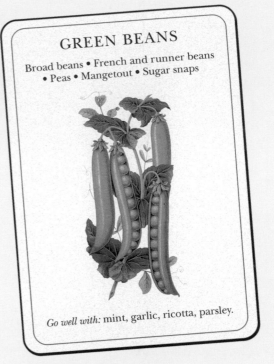

*Go well with:* mint, garlic, ricotta, parsley.

## SOFT LEAVES

Spinach • Chard • Beet leaves

*Go well with* garlic, chillies, olive oil, eggs, vegetarian Parmesan-style cheese.

## NIGHTSHADES

Tomatoes • Aubergines • Peppers • Courgettes*

*\* Not strictly a nightshade but an honorary member of the family for culinary purposes*

*Go well with* mint, basil, oregano, vinegar, capers, mozzarella, chillies.

## SWEET & ORANGE

Squash • Sweet potato • Pumpkin

*Go well with* garlic, sage, rosemary, chillies, coconut, coriander, lime, blue cheese, pecans.

## ALLIUMS

Onions • Leeks
• Spring Onions • Garlic

*Go well with* sage, vegetarian Parmesan-style cheese, balsamic vinegar.

## POPULAR ROOTS

Carrots • Parsnips • Celeriac
• Fennel** • Celery**

*Go well with* mayonnaise, cumin, lemon, olives, mustard.

** *Both honorary members*

## BRASSICA HEADS

Broccoli • Cauliflower • Romanesco

*Go well with* almonds, chives, cheese, capers, mustard.

## NEGLECTED ROOTS

Turnips • Beetroot
• Jerusalem artichokes • Swede

*Go well with* caraway, orange, hazelnuts, vinegar, butter, sage, parsley.

## BRASSICAS

Cabbages • Sprouts • Kale
• Spring greens

*Go well with* caraway, almonds, pine nuts, chillies, garlic, fontina (or other melting cheese).

# Tips & Techniques for Prepping Vegetables

- Keep your work surface tidy. Have a large bowl to hand: peel vegetables over it and lob in any trimmings.

- Soak onions in cold water for 20 minutes to make them easier to peel.

- Soak garlic cloves in very hot water for 30 minutes. The skins should then slip off easily.

- If you are going to use garlic in a dressing, or if it's hardly going to be cooked, chop it first and then, using the flat of your knife and a sprinkling of salt, crush it to a paste. That way you should benefit from the flavour without eating a massive raw chunk.

- Use a teaspoon to peel particularly knobbly fresh ginger.

- Some people find preparing pumpkins, squashes and celeriac very challenging. The best way to deal with them is to cut them into sections with a large knife and then peel the skin off each section with a peeler or serrated tomato knife.

- Jerusalem artichokes (or nobbly bobblies, as they are fondly known) can be a bit of a nightmare to peel. If they are relatively clean and the skin is not too thick, peeling isn't necessary, but give them a very good wash. If you do need to peel them, use a tomato knife instead of a speed peeler and put them straight into water with a little lemon juice added to stop them discolouring.

- It is also not necessary to peel good-quality and young carrots … a good wash or scrub will do.

- To skin tomatoes, make a cross with a knife at the base of each one and place them in boiling water. Leave for 30 seconds, then drain and refresh in cold water. The skins should come off easily.

- To peel red peppers, toss them in a little olive oil and place in a very hot oven for 10–15 minutes, until slightly charred. Alternatively, the peppers can be charred under a grill, on a naked flame or on a charcoal grill. Transfer immediately to a bowl, cover with clingfilm (or tie them into a plastic food bag) and leave them until cool. When cool, peel off the skins.

# Common Mistakes & Culinary First Aid

- To avoid any problems when following a recipe, read it through first – you may need to soak an ingredient beforehand, for example. Get a good idea of how to proceed, and make sure you have the right ingredients and equipment.

- It is very important to taste your food as you are cooking. This is essential in order for you to gauge how the flavours are developing, and because it will become evident if you have over-seasoned or over-spiced.

- Remember that something can almost always be salvaged from a disaster, and that occasionally this is how new dishes are created.

- Even the most experienced chefs will sometimes burn the bottom of a pan. If this happens, do not mix the burnt bits in with whatever you are cooking. Remove the pan from the heat, carefully decant the contents into a clean pan, leaving behind all the burnt areas, and carry on.

- If a dish is too spicy, add some yoghurt or coconut milk. A little honey or vinegar can also temper the heat.

- Over-salting is a common problem – we all have a different salt tolerance, often depending on the food we are used to. Adding some slices of raw potato to a soup or sauce can help remove some of the saltiness; cook until the potatoes are translucent, then remove them. Rice puréed with water can also be added to temper saltiness. A dash of vinegar, brown sugar or cream is also worth trying.

- Know your oven. Every oven, even the most sophisticated, seems to have its hottest and coolest parts. This is particularly important when baking.

- If you are worried about overcooking a green vegetable like asparagus for a special dinner, blanch it beforehand for 2 minutes in boiling water, then refresh in iced water. Drain and set aside. Just before serving, warm through in a little warm olive oil or butter.

- To prevent a cake mixture from splitting, make sure your eggs are at room temperature before adding them. Cold eggs straight from the fridge are much more likely to split.

- Eggs at room temperature are also important when making mayonnaise from scratch. If your mayo does separate, use another egg yolk as a base and add your split mixture to it slowly, whisking continuously.

- To avoid a split hollandaise, have your melted butter and egg yolks at about the same temperature before whisking them together. If they do separate, remove them from the heat and try whisking in an ice cube. If this fails, use another egg yolk to bring it back, as with mayonnaise above.

# Using Leftovers

The art of 'good housekeeping' is making sure that nothing is wasted. Certain cultures have it down to a fine art – the Italians, for example, being particularly brilliant with stale bread, while the British can boast one of the greatest leftover dishes: bubble and squeak.

## MASH / PURÉES

❀ Add chopped cooked kale to the mash and season with herbs and mustard. Shape into patties and fry in butter.

❀ For bubble and squeak, add some mashed swede to the potato mash, along with finely shredded cooked sprouts or cabbage. Fry in a large non-stick pan in butter and oil.

❀ To make potato croquettes (pictured), beat an egg yolk and some melted butter into the mash. Form into small cylinder shapes. Coat them first in flour, then in beaten egg, then in breadcrumbs, and deep-fry until golden.

❀ The same can be done with creamed parsnips, but use chopped almonds instead of breadcrumbs.

CROQUETTES

## STALE BREAD

❀ The Italians are masters of turning stale bread into something wonderful, for example Ribollita (see page 56) and Salvatore's Panzanella (see page 77).

❀ Toasting pieces of stale ciabatta or pitta bread and tossing them in a salad dressing while warm makes a great base for any salad. Add other ingredients when cool.

❀ Stale bread makes great croûtons or a base for bruschetta.

❀ And there's always bread pudding!

## POTATOES

❀ Dice cooked potatoes and add to fried mustard seeds, curry leaves and spices to make Bombay potatoes.

❀ Cut leftover baked potatoes in half and scoop out the flesh. Mix with grated cheese, an egg yolk, cooked chopped leeks or onions and chopped herbs. Pile the mixture back into the skins and cook in a preheated oven at 180°C/350°F/gas mark 4 for 10–15 minutes.

## RICE

✿ **Arancini** (pictured): A great snack to serve at parties or as a starter using cooked risotto rice. They are particularly delicious made with squash risotto or porcini mushroom risotto. Roll leftover risotto into walnut-shaped balls and press in a little lump of mozzarella (or blue cheese). Coat them first in flour, then in beaten egg, then in breadcrumbs, and deep-fry until golden.

✿ **Al salto**: Fry leftover risotto in butter in an ovenproof frying pan, pressing it down to make a cake. Bake in a medium oven for about 15 minutes, then turn it out on to a plate and cut into wedges to serve.

✿ **Stir-fry**: In a wok, stir-fry leftover cooked rice with chilli, basil and garlic and any vegetables of your choosing, for 5 minutes over a high heat. Finish with a dash of soy sauce.

✿ **Soups**: Add leftover cooked rice to soup 3 minutes before serving.

ARANCINI

## CHEESE

✿ Cook sliced leeks in butter and grate in any manky bits of cheese you have around. Use as a topping for toast or on a pizza base. Cook in a hot oven for 5 minutes.

## FRITTATA

✿ A great way to use up roasted or blanched vegetables – add them to slow-cooked onions and beaten eggs and cook in a deep frying pan. Leftover spaghetti can be chopped and added, too.

## SALAD

❀ Little Gems, iceberg, etc – make a great lettuce soup. Fry chopped onions and leeks in butter until soft. Add roughly chopped lettuce and cook until wilted. Pour in hot vegetable stock, bring to the boil, then blend. Fresh herbs or vegetarian Parmesan-style cheese can be added just before serving.

❀ Toss chopped rocket through pasta with tomato sauce and grate over some hard ricotta or feta.

## SFORMATO

❀ Blend leftover cooked cauliflower, broccoli and spinach to a pulp. Mix with eggs, milk and a little flour. Season well and add grated cheese. The resulting batter is baked in a preheated oven at 160°C/325°F/gas mark 3 until firm, but with a slight wobble.

❀ Cauliflower (or broccoli) cheese can easily be turned into a delicious soup by adding vegetable stock and/or milk and blending.

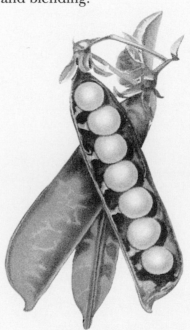

## VINAIGRETTE

Most cold blanched vegetables, such as broccoli, French beans, runner beans, mangetout and sugar snap peas, will make a great addition to a salad, either with a basic vinaigrette or one of the dressings from pages 198–99 or 202.

## SOUP

❀ Most cooked vegetables can be turned into a soup by chopping them finely and adding them to a base of sweated, diced onions, leeks, carrots and celery, and a good vegetable stock (see opposite). The longer you cook this *soffrito*, the better the resulting soup. To make a more substantial meal, add some herbs and small cooked pasta such as orzo, ditalini or macaroni.

# Vegetable Stock

Although stocks can be made from scraps and peelings, it is worth investing in high-quality vegetables to make a really good vegetable stock.

1 tablespoon **olive oil**

2 **onions**, finely chopped

2 sticks of **celery**, finely chopped

2 **carrots**, finely chopped

1 **leek**, chopped

1 slice of **swede**, chopped

150g **mushrooms**, sliced

150g **tomatoes**, chopped (fresh or tinned)

3 cloves of **garlic**, crushed

1 **bay leaf**

**parsley** stalks

1 tablespoon **black peppercorns**

1. Heat the oil in a large pan and add the onions, celery, carrots, leeks and swede.

2. Fry gently for 5 minutes, then add the rest of the ingredients and 1.25 litres of cold water.

3. Bring to the boil, then reduce the heat and simmer for an hour. Strain.

# PART ONE

# STAR TURNS

LEON

**FULL OF SUN**

Dishes that can stand alone
as a whole meal

# BREAKFAST & BRUNCH

LEON

# Leon Baked Beans

SERVES 6 • PREPARATION TIME: 5 MINUTES • COOKING TIME: 15 MINUTES • ♥ WF GF DF V

A Leon favourite. We serve these on our poached eggs in the morning and with our full English breakfast pot.

1 tablespoon **olive oil**

1 **onion**, finely chopped

1 tablespoon **tomato purée**

200g tinned **chopped tomatoes**

a pinch of **sugar**

2 x 300g tins of **haricot beans**, drained

100ml **water**

**salt** and **freshly ground black pepper**

1. Heat the olive oil in a large pan, then add the onion and cook over a medium heat for 5 minutes, or until soft.

2. Add the tomato purée, tomatoes and sugar, stir well to combine, then cook quickly for 5 minutes over a high heat.

3. Stir in the drained beans and lower the heat to medium. Cook for another 5 minutes, adding the water to prevent the beans sticking. Season well before serving.

**TIPS**

* The beans themselves can be added to stews or Roast Mixed Roots (see page 238) to make a heartier dish.

* Loads of different seasonings can be added to this basic bean recipe. Here are some suggestions:

  • Smoked paprika (to taste)
  • 2 teaspoons of molasses and a little balsamic vinegar
  • Chopped fresh chilli, garlic and/or parsley

LEON, NITA, TIM, MARION AND JOE, PORTUGAL 1964

# Pancakey Pie

Making the pancakes ahead of time and soaking the porcini early will speed up this method.

**FOR THE PANCAKES**

1 **egg**

50ml **water**

200ml **milk**

70g **plain flour**, sifted

**salt** and **freshly ground black pepper**

a little **butter**, plus extra for greasing

**FOR THE FILLING**

30g **dried porcini**

300ml **boiling water**

1 tablespoon **olive oil**

1 clove of **garlic**, crushed

a sprig of **fresh thyme**

300g **mushrooms**, finely chopped

1 tablespoon **crème fraîche**

1 **egg**

1 tablespoon **vegetarian Parmesan-style cheese**

**TIPS**

\* Try this with different types of mushrooms and herbs.

This dish was invented by my old chef at the Field Kitchen, Ben Bulger, as a vegetarian special ... we were filmed making it together and it has become a very, very minor YouTube sensation!

JANE

BEN, AT HIS GRANDPA'S, BRISTOL, 1982

1. Put the porcini into a bowl and pour over the boiling water. Leave to soak for 30 minutes.

2. Heat the oven to 180°C/350°F/gas mark 4.

3. Put the egg into a bowl with the water and milk and whisk together until smooth. Put the flour into a second bowl and slowly add the egg mixture, whisking to make a smooth batter. Season.

4. Melt a little butter in a non-stick pan over a medium heat. Slowly pour in some of the batter and tilt the pan until the whole base is lightly coated. Cook for 1 minute, then flip over to the other side. Cook for another minute, then tip the pancake out of the pan on to a sheet of baking paper. Repeat with the rest of the mixture – it should make 6 pancakes.

5. Drain the porcini, reserving the soaking liquid, and chop finely. Heat the olive oil in a frying pan, add the porcini and cook over a medium heat for 1 minute. Add the garlic and thyme, stir, and pour in the reserved porcini liquid. Turn up the heat and cook until the liquid has reduced to a few tablespoons.

6. Add the chopped mushrooms and cook for 5 minutes over a high heat, until they are tender. Remove the pan from the heat and allow to cool until tepid. Season well.

7. Whisk together the crème fraîche, egg and Parmesan and stir into the mushroom mixture.

8. To assemble, grease a 24cm springform cake tin and line it with baking paper. Place 1 pancake in the bottom of the tin and spread with one-fifth of the mushroom mixture. Top with another pancake and repeat the process until all the mixture and pancakes are used up, finishing with a pancake on top.

9. Bake in the oven for about 20 minutes. Allow to cool slightly, then remove the tin and cut into wedges to serve.

# Asparagus & Wild Garlic Frittata

SERVES 4 • PREPARATION TIME: 10 MINUTES • COOKING TIME: 10 MINUTES • WF GF V

Asparagus and wild garlic have roughly the same season, and this is a simple brunch using both. Fresh mint or basil can be used instead of the garlic leaves.

350–400g **asparagus**

6 **eggs**

1 tablespoon **white wine**

2 tablespoons grated vegetarian **pecorino or Parmesan-style cheese**

**salt** and **freshly ground black pepper**

1 tablespoon **olive oil**

1 clove of **garlic**, crushed

1 small bunch of **wild garlic leaves**, washed and shredded

1. To prepare the asparagus, first snap off and discard the woody ends. Cut the asparagus into 2–3cm lengths. Bring a large pan of salted water to the boil, add the asparagus, blanch for 2 minutes and drain.

2. Put the eggs into a bowl with the white wine and 1 tablespoon of grated pecorino and whisk together. Season well.

3. Heat the grill. Heat the olive oil in a 22–24cm non-stick frying pan. Add the asparagus, garlic and wild garlic leaves and sauté over a medium heat for 2 minutes, then lower the heat.

4. Pour in the egg mixture and draw in from the sides with a wooden spoon to allow the uncooked egg to run underneath.

5. Cook gently for 5 minutes. Sprinkle with the rest of the cheese and flash under the hot grill to finish cooking the top.

6. Slide from the pan on to a large plate and cut into wedges to serve.

**VARIATIONS**

❀ Purple sprouting broccoli can be substituted for the asparagus.

❀ Try using diced aubergine or courgettes, but do not cook them in boiling water – instead sauté them lightly in olive oil before adding to the egg mix.

❀ Sautéd onions and red peppers make a delicious frittata, so cook them with a little vinegar and sugar and add lots of shredded basil to the egg mix.

**TIPS**

* This is lovely served hot, but is also good at room temperature.

* If you have any leftover cooked Jersey Royals, slice them up and drop them in the mix.

# Fonduta

## WITH PURPLE SPROUTING BROCCOLI & ASPARAGUS

SERVES 4 • PREPARATION TIME: 10 MINUTES • COOKING TIME: 20 MINUTES • ✓ WF GF V

This northern Italian fondue typically uses fontina cheese, but you can substitute with Gruyère or a vegetarian cheese with the same melting qualities.

50g **butter**

175ml **milk**

220g **fontina cheese**, grated

3 large **egg yolks**

250g **asparagus spears**

250g **purple sprouting broccoli spears**

**salt** and **freshly ground black pepper**

1. Melt the butter in a double boiler (or in a bowl sitting over a pan of simmering water).

2. Meanwhile, in a separate bowl, whisk together the milk, cheese and egg yolks.

3. Slowly add the milk and cheese mixture to the melted butter and whisk continuously over the heat until it thickens, then remove from the heat.

4. Bring a pan of salted water to the boil and cook the asparagus for 2–3 minutes, until tender. Remove from the pan and repeat with the purple sprouting broccoli.

5. Season the fonduta and serve in a bowl surrounded by the vegetables – ready to dip.

I first heard of this dish while working at The River Café, but I had never tasted it in its native Piedmont until I went on a truffle hunt with Henry and a bunch of chefs. On our three-day 'truffle immersion' we tried it in various different restaurants, my favourite version being served with an egg yolk and topped with lots of shaved white truffles. Another great dish involved the fonduta sauce being poured over cooked cardoon stalks, with, yet again, lots of shaved truffles on top, but served in cute individual fondue-like bowls over a warming tea-light – apparatus that appeared to be standard in most Italian establishments.

JANE

JANE, AGE 2, IN BACK GARDEN, SUNDERLAND

**VARIATIONS**

✿ Try using a little smoked cheese in the fonduta, or a blue cheese like Gorgonzola.

✿ Drizzle the fonduta with a little truffle oil or truffle honey.

# Scrambled Tofu

SERVES 4 • PREPARATION TIME: 15 MINUTES • COOKING TIME: 15 MINUTES • ♥ ✓ WF GF DF V

There are some doubters among us when it comes to this dish, but please try it – you will be surprised. It makes a satisfying breakfast for even the most ardent tofu hater. It is traditionally served on toast, but stands as a dish on its own, too.

2 tablespoons **olive oil**

1 **onion**, finely chopped

1 **chilli**, finely chopped

1 **red pepper**, finely chopped

a pinch of **ground turmeric**

a pinch of **ground cumin**

200g **mixed vegetables**
(broccoli florets, cauliflower
florets, peas, spinach)

300g **tofu**

4 **cherry tomatoes**,
cut into quarters

a drizzle of **soy sauce**

**salt** and **freshly ground
black pepper**

**OPTIONAL TOPPINGS**

**spring onions**, chopped

**fresh coriander**, chopped

1. Heat the olive oil in a frying pan, then add the onion, chilli, red pepper and spices and cook over a medium heat for 5 minutes.

2. Bring a pan of salted water to the boil and quickly cook the mixed vegetables for 3 minutes (if including spinach or other leaves, add them just before draining). Drain the vegetables and set aside.

3. Crumble the tofu into the onion mixture and stir well.

4. Add the drained vegetables and tomatoes, stir and cook for another 3 minutes over a medium heat.

5. Finish off the dish with a dash of soy sauce to taste, season well, and serve, sprinkled with spring onions and/or fresh coriander, if using.

I first tried this dish in Byron Bay, Australia – the resort is full of cafés and restaurants, with lots of competition at breakfast and brunch. Byron Bay these days is a very popular surfy holiday place, but years ago it was a hippy alternative retreat and there are signs of this everywhere – possibly because of this, the scrambled tofu lives on. This dish should really be mainstream and up there with poached eggs on toast … honest.

JANE

**TIPS**

* Follow the same method above but try adding 3 beaten eggs instead of the tofu, then scramble as normal, adding your blanched vegetables at the end of cooking.

* For very quick spiced scrambled eggs, fry the turmeric, chopped chilli and a few cumin seeds in the oil for a minute. Add 3 beaten eggs and cook, stirring gently, over a medium heat until almost set. Season well and finish with lots of chopped coriander.

# Baxter's Brunch

SERVES 4 • PREPARATION TIME: 5 MINUTES • COOKING TIME: 10 MINUTES • V

You can't beat eggs on toast. This is Jane's favourite breakfast.

4 slices of **sourdough bread**
(or other good-quality bread)

1 clove of **garlic**, cut in half

good **olive oil**

**Marmite**, for spreading

4 slices of **fontina or
Gruyère cheese**

4 **eggs**

a splash of **white wine vinegar**

8 **cherry tomatoes**, sliced

2 **red chillies**,
deseeded and chopped

**salt** and **freshly ground
black pepper**

1. Toast the bread, either in a toaster or on a preheated griddle pan. Rub each side with the garlic and drizzle with olive oil.

2. Spread each slice with Marmite and top with the cheese. Put on a baking tray and set aside while you poach the eggs.

3. Heat the grill. Bring a large pan of water to the boil, then reduce to a simmer. Add the vinegar, then gently slide in the eggs and poach them for 2 minutes, or until they are cooked but still have a runny yolk. Remove with a slotted spoon and drain on kitchen paper.

4. Place the baking tray of toast under a hot grill until the cheese is bubbling, then put on serving plates.

5. Put some of the tomatoes on top of each toast, then a poached egg, followed by a sprinkling of chilli and a drizzle of oil. Season well and serve.

**TIPS**

* The fresher the egg, the better the results when poaching.

* If you crack your eggs into a small cup and lower them gently into the simmering water, the egg will have a more professional-looking finish.

* You can poach the eggs ahead of time and transfer to iced water to stop them cooking. Before serving, immerse them in boiling water for 30 seconds to heat through.

The original version of this super breakfast is one that we used to eat in the morning while deciding on our menu at The River Café. It was created by Rose Grey and has long since been my favourite brekkie, although her version used an anchovy sauce that we would always have in the fridge (either bagna cauda or anchovy and rosemary) instead of the Marmite.

JANE

JANE, AGE 4, BACKHOUSE PARK, SUNDERLAND

# Cinnamon Toasts

## WITH RHUBARB & ORANGE COMPOTE & HONEYED YOGHURT

SERVES 4 • PREPARATION TIME: 20 MINUTES • COOKING TIME: 15 MINUTES • V Ⓥ

For an indulgent breakfast or brunch.

4 thick slices of **white bread**

30g softened **butter**,
for spreading

4 teaspoons **caster sugar**

2 teaspoons **ground cinnamon**

**honey**, to taste

4 tablespoons **Greek yoghurt**

1. Preheat the grill. Toast the bread lightly and butter generously on both sides. Leave the grill on, or heat a griddle pan until it is very hot.

2. Mix together the sugar and cinnamon and sprinkle on both sides of the toast.

3. Either flash the toast quickly under the hot grill to brown on both sides, or brown both sides in the hot griddle pan.

4. Stir a little honey into the yoghurt and serve with the toasts, alongside some Rhubarb & Orange Compote (see below).

# Rhubarb & Orange Compote

SERVES 4 • PREPARATION TIME: 5 MINUTES • COOKING TIME: 10 MINUTES • WF GF DF V

200g **rhubarb**, trimmed and
cut into 2cm pieces

125g **caster sugar**

1 tablespoon **grenadine**

50ml **water**

juice and grated zest of
2 **oranges**

2 **oranges**, segmented

1. Put the rhubarb, sugar, grenadine, water, orange juice and zest into a pan. Cook gently over a medium heat for 10 minutes, or until the rhubarb is soft.

2. Remove from the heat, transfer to a serving bowl and top with orange segments.

### TIPS

* To be less decadent, use wholemeal bread.

* Cut your toast into hearts (as we have) because things like that should be done more often.

* Try stirring your compote into a steaming bowl of porridge.

* The compote is also good to serve as a dessert, as an accompaniment to panna cotta or a custard tart.

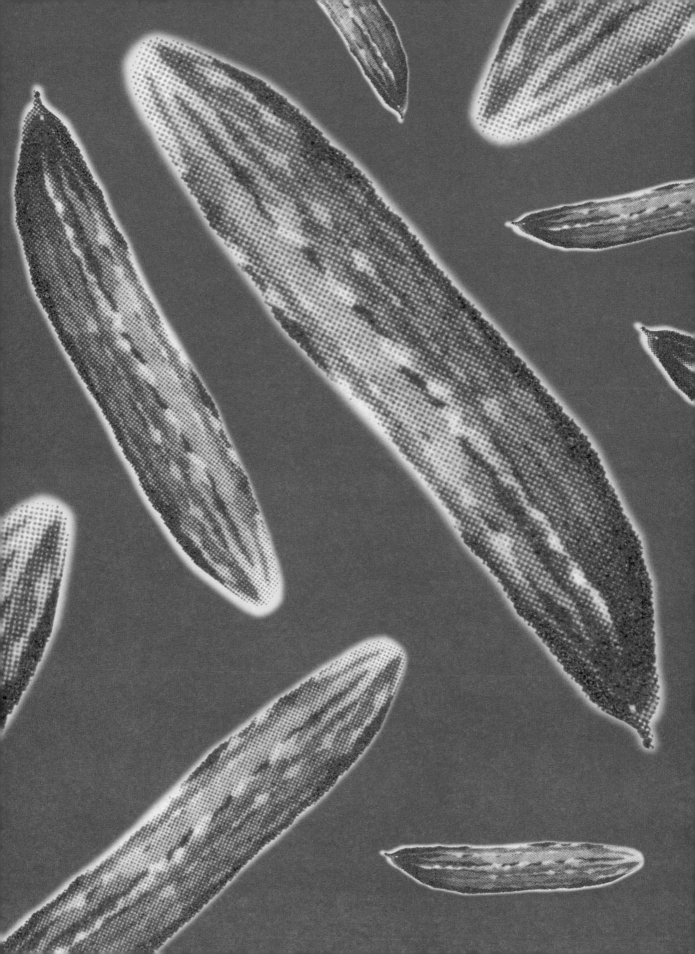

# SOUP

LEON

# Gazpacho

SERVES 2 • PREPARATION TIME: 10 MINUTES • COOKING TIME: NONE • ♥ ✓ WF GF DF V

This recipe does not involve deseeding and peeling the tomatoes, but for a smoother result, pass the gazpacho through a mouli-légumes (or a food mill).

1–2 **green peppers**, deseeded

8 juicy red **tomatoes**

1 **cucumber**, peeled

4 cloves of **garlic**, crushed

4 tablespoons very good **olive oil**

2 tablespoons **white wine vinegar**

**salt**

1. Put all the ingredients into a liquidizer and blend together until smooth.

2. Check the seasoning, and add more olive oil or vinegar according to taste.

3. Transfer to a bowl and chill for at least 2 hours, longer if possible – this soup will definitely improve with keeping.

DAVID, 1972

JO ON A BEACH IN JERSEY, WITH HER PARENTS, 1972

This recipe was given to me by my friends Dave and Jo who acquired it while on holiday in Spain. It is a traditional, simple gazpacho that they like to make with powerful amounts of garlic and vinegar. I like it like this, but you should experiment with the quantities as you like. Incidentally, I think that gazpacho is one of the few worthwhile uses for a green pepper.

HENRY

**TIPS**

* If you want to serve it quickly, add a few ice cubes to the mix before you blend it.

# Chilled Cucumber Soup

SERVES 4 • PREPARATION TIME: 10 MINUTES • COOKING TIME: NONE • ♥ ✓ WF GF V

A lovely, quick, cooling soup for a hot summer's day ... let's hope we have some of those.

1kg **cucumbers**, peeled and deseeded

½ a **red onion**, finely chopped

2 cloves of **garlic**, crushed

1 **green chilli**, deseeded and chopped

2 tablespoons chopped **fresh mint leaves**

juice of 1 **lemon**

2 teaspoons **honey**

50ml **olive oil**

150g **natural yoghurt**

100–150ml **water**

**salt**

1. Put all the ingredients into a food processor and blend until the soup is very smooth. If necessary, add more water to thin the soup down to your desired consistency.

2. Transfer to a bowl and chill for at least 2 hours before serving.

ALWAYS WEAR YOUR BUOYANCY DEVICE WHEN EATING SOUP NEAR A BODY OF WATER

# Wild Garlic, Potato & Almond Soup

SERVES 4 • PREPARATION TIME: 10 MINUTES • COOKING TIME: 30 MINUTES • ♥ WF GF DF V

In shady lanes and woodlands during May there is an abundance of wild garlic leaves to pick. This lovely soup makes good use of these leaves and brings some green and freshness to a time of year known as the 'hunger gap', before the influx of summer vegetables.

2 tablespoons **olive oil**

1 **onion**, chopped

1 **leek**, white and pale green parts, chopped

2 cloves of **garlic**, crushed

400g **floury potatoes**, peeled and cut into small pieces

1 litre **vegetable stock**

100g **wild garlic leaves**

75g toasted **flaked almonds**

**salt** and **freshly ground black pepper**

**OPTIONAL GARNISH**

**crème fraîche**

**flaked almonds**

**extra virgin olive oil**

1. Heat the olive oil in a large pan, then add the onion and leeks and cook over a medium heat for 10 minutes.

2. Add the garlic and stir well, then add the potatoes. Mix well, then reduce the heat to low and cook for 5 minutes.

3. Pour in the vegetable stock and bring to the boil. Turn the heat down to a simmer and cook for 10 minutes, or until the potatoes are tender.

4. Wash and roughly chop the garlic leaves and add to the soup. Simmer for a further 2 minutes.

5. Stir in the almonds, then blend the soup in batches until smooth.

6. Season well and serve, either just as it is or with a blob of crème fraîche, a sprinkling of almonds and a drizzle of olive oil. Or you could really push the boat out and sprinkle each serving with some wild garlic flowers.

**TIPS**

* Some greengrocers now sell wild garlic. If you can't find it, spinach and lots of herbs like chives and tarragon can be used along with more crushed garlic.

* Toasted hazelnuts make a richer substitute for the almonds.

* Serve this over a very garlicky grilled bruschetta.

WILD GARLIC IN THE GROUND

A FARMER AT SHUMEI FARM, YATESBURY IN WILTSHIRE, PLOUGHING THE FIELDS.

# Rasam

SERVES 6 • PREPARATION TIME: 10 MINUTES • COOKING TIME: 40 MINUTES • ♥ ✓ WF GF DF V

Rasam is a South Indian soup that can be eaten either with rice or on its own.

50g **red lentils**

1 teaspoon **black peppercorns**

2 teaspoons **cumin seeds**

3 **dried red chillies**

2 cloves of **garlic**, crushed

750g ripe **tomatoes**, chopped

1 tablespoon **sunflower oil**

1 teaspoon **mustard seeds**

10 **curry leaves**

a pinch of **ground turmeric**

2 teaspoons **tamarind paste**

750ml **water**

**salt** and **freshly ground black pepper**

**TIPS**

* A blob of yoghurt and some chopped fresh coriander may be used to finish this soup.

1. Wash the lentils and put them into a pan. Cover them with water and cook over a medium heat for 20 minutes, or until soft. Remove from the heat and set aside.

2. Dry-roast the peppercorns, cumin seeds and chillies in a small frying pan over a medium heat for 2 minutes. Grind them together in a pestle and mortar or let them cool a little and grind in a spice grinder to a powder. Mix them with the crushed garlic to form a paste, then set aside.

3. Blend the tomatoes in a liquidizer or food processor.

4. Heat the oil in a large pan and add the mustard seeds and curry leaves. Cook over a medium heat until the seeds start to pop, then add the tomatoes and turmeric.

5. Add the lentils, spice paste, tamarind and water and bring to a simmer. Cook over a low heat for 15 minutes, then pass through a sieve or food mill. Season well and serve.

# Spiced Farro Soup

SERVES 4–6 • PREPARATION TIME: 5 MINUTES • COOKING TIME: 45 MINUTES • ♥ WF GF DF V

Farro is often used in Italy in salads and soups. It needs to be soaked for 4 hours before cooking in this recipe, to speed up the cooking process. This is a hearty soup for a chilly day, and cooked beans or chickpeas can be added too, to make it even more substantial.

200g **farro**

1 tablespoon **olive oil**

1 **onion**, finely chopped

2 cloves of **garlic**, chopped

1 **dried chilli**, chopped

**salt** and **freshly ground black pepper**

1 litre **vegetable stock**

1 x 440g tin of **chopped tomatoes**

**extra virgin olive oil**

1. Put the farro into a bowl and cover with plenty of cold water. Leave to soak for 4 hours, then drain.

2. Heat the oil in a large pan and add the onion, garlic and chilli. Cook for 5 minutes over a medium heat.

3. Add the drained farro, season and stir, then pour in half the stock. Bring to a simmer and cook gently for 20 minutes.

4. Add the tomatoes and the rest of the stock and season well. Simmer for a further 20 minutes.

5. Remove half the soup and blend in a liquidizer or food processor, then stir it back into the soup in the pan, together with a good drizzle of olive oil. Serve.

**TIPS**

* If you do not serve this soup straight away the farro will continue to absorb the liquid, so you will need to add extra stock when reheating.

* Chopped fresh rosemary or sage can be added with the onion.

CHRISTINE (ROCKING THE DUNGAREES) AGE 2, KENT

I am very lucky to have had the opportunity to work and travel to Italy with Christine Smallwood, author of *An Appetite for Umbria* and *An Appetite for Puglia*. She is a font of knowledge on these regions, especially on the restaurateurs and food producers, and has greatly influenced my work. She is currently working on the next books in her Italian series, including the region of Lombardy.

JANE

# Corn Chowder

SERVES 4 • PREPARATION TIME: 15 MINUTES • COOKING TIME: 40 MINUTES • WF GF V

Another soup for an autumn evening, when corn is plentiful and the nights are drawing in.

50g **butter**

2 **onions**, finely chopped

2 cloves of **garlic**, crushed

2 **red chillies**, chopped

a sprig of **fresh thyme** (or a pinch of dried thyme)

a good pinch of **ground cumin**

a good pinch of **smoked paprika**

1 **red pepper**, finely chopped

4 cobs of **sweetcorn**

2 **baking potatoes** (about 400g), peeled and cut into 1cm dice

a splash of **white wine** (about 50ml)

500ml **milk** (soya milk can be used)

250ml **water**

**salt** and **freshly ground black pepper**

1. Melt the butter in a large pan over a low heat. Add the onions, garlic, chillies, thyme, spices and red pepper and cook for 10 minutes, stirring occasionally.

2. Remove the kernels from the sweetcorn cobs by standing them upright on a chopping board and cutting downwards with a sawing action. Add the kernels to the pan and turn up the heat, stirring constantly for 5 minutes so that the corn browns slightly, but be careful not to let it burn.

3. Add the diced potatoes, followed by the wine, and turn up the heat. Cook rapidly for 1 minute.

4. Pour in the milk and bring to a simmer. Cook over a low heat for 10 minutes, then add the water, bring back to a simmer and continue to cook for a further 10 minutes, or until the potatoes are tender and the soup begins to thicken. Season well and serve.

### TIPS

* Cooked spinach or chard can be added to this soup in the final stages.

* Chopped fresh parsley or coriander adds a lovely finishing touch.

**BY AIRMAIL**
**PAR AVION**

One of my favourite corn recipes is Sean Moran's creamed corn, from his restaurant on Bondi Beach in Sydney. The chowder above has the same flavours, and uses the same method to bring out the sweetness of the corn; caramelizing it in the butter mix without burning it before adding the liquid.

JANE

# Sweet Potato, Orange & Cardamom Soup

SERVES 4 • PREPARATION TIME: 10 MINUTES • COOKING TIME: 30 MINUTES • ♥ ✓ WF GF DF V

A fragrant, stunningly coloured soup.

1 tablespoon **olive oil**

I **red onion**, finely chopped

approx. 600g **sweet potatoes**

2 cloves of **garlic**, crushed

seeds from 2 **cardamom pods**, crushed

1 litre **vegetable stock**

juice of 1 **orange**

**salt** and **freshly ground black pepper**

1. Heat the olive oil in a large pan over a medium heat, then add the red onion and cook for 5 minutes.

2. Peel the sweet potatoes, then cut them into quarters lengthways and thinly slice each quarter. Add to the onions with the garlic and cardamom and cook for a further 5 minutes.

3. Add the vegetable stock and bring to the boil. Reduce the heat and simmer for 15 minutes, or until the sweet potatoes are soft. Blend with an immersion blender until smooth.

4. Add the orange juice, season to taste, then serve.

**TIPS**

* Chickpeas can be added for more substance.

* Replacing some of the sweet potatoes with carrots will make it slightly lighter.

* Finish the soup with a little cream or crème fraîche.

DAVID, AGE 5, PUB, ST MARTINS, SCILLY ISLES

# Ribollita

SERVES 4 • PREPARATION TIME: 15 MINUTES • COOKING TIME: 25 MINUTES • ♥ ✓ DF V

This is a hearty Tuscan soup that literally means 'reboiled'. It is a creative way of using up stale bread, something the Italians do so well. If you have time to cook the vegetables for longer at the start, the soup will be better for it.

2 tablespoons **olive oil**

1 **onion**, finely chopped

3 sticks of **celery**, finely chopped

1 large **carrot**, chopped

a pinch of **dried chilli**

a pinch of **wild oregano** (optional)

3 cloves of **garlic**, crushed

¼ of a **Savoy cabbage** (or other cabbage), cored and shredded

1 x 400g tin of **chopped tomatoes**

**salt** and **freshly ground black pepper**

1 x 400g tin of **borlotti beans** (or white beans), drained

300g **black kale**, de-stemmed and shredded

400ml **boiling water**

200g stale **ciabatta**, broken into 2–3cm chunks

**extra virgin olive oil**, to serve

**TIPS**

* The base for this soup makes a good minestrone, so you could add cooked small pasta or macaroni instead of the bread.

* For a great side dish, leave out the bread, water, braised kale and beans.

1. Heat the olive oil in a large pan and add the onion, celery and carrot. Cook for 10 minutes over a low heat, then add the chilli, oregano and garlic and cook for 2 more minutes, stirring well.

2. Add the shredded cabbage and tomatoes, season, stir well and cook over a high heat for 5 minutes.

3. Add the beans and shredded kale and pour in the boiling water. Stir, then bring to a simmer and cook for another 5 minutes, or until the kale is tender.

4. Remove a cupful of the soup and blend well in a liquidizer or food processor, then stir it back into the soup in the pan.

5. Bring the soup back to a simmer, then remove from the heat and fold in the chunks of bread. Drizzle with lots of extra virgin olive oil, check the seasoning and serve.

# Spinach & Lentil Soup

SERVES 4 • PREPARATION TIME: 10 MINUTES • COOKING TIME: 35 MINUTES • ♥ ✓ WF GF DF V

This is a great healthy soup that can either be served on its own or can be transformed by the addition of other ingredients.

1 tablespoon **olive oil**

1 **onion**, finely chopped

1 **leek**, finely chopped

1 stick of **celery**, finely chopped

3 cloves of **garlic**, crushed

200g **Puy lentils** (or other green lentils)

1 litre **water**

300g **spinach**, large stalks removed and leaves washed

**salt** and **freshly ground black pepper**

a drizzle of **olive oil**

1. Heat the oil in a large pan and add the onion, leek and celery. Cook slowly over a medium heat for 10 minutes.

2. Add the garlic and lentils and cook for 2 minutes, then pour in the water.

3. Bring to a simmer and cook gently over a low heat for 20 minutes, or until the lentils are tender.

4. Roughly chop the spinach and add to the soup. Cook for 1 minute, until the spinach has wilted.

5. Remove half the soup and blend in a liquidizer or food processor until smooth, then stir it back into the soup in the pan.

6. Season well, and serve with a drizzle of olive oil.

**VARIATIONS**

❀ Try adding some diced squash, fennel seeds and dried chilli when you add the garlic and lentils before continuing with the recipe.

❀ For a southern Indian flavour, add ground cumin, coriander and cardamom when you add the garlic and lentils, then finish with a grating of creamed coconut.

# Snickety Corner – The Fridge Buffet

These ideas are inspired by Oisin Rogers, who runs The Ship in Wandsworth and The Thatched House in Hammersmith, London. He has been banned by his wife from cooking when he gets in late at night, so instead he makes himself ingenious cold snacks from the fridge – the fridge buffet. You can read all about them if you follow him on Twitter. Here are some of his favourites, as well as some from other people who've worked on this book.

## OISIN

From the master of fridge snackage, these are quite sophisticated but involve no cooking/heating.

* Caperberries, sliced sunblush tomato and apple with mayo on rye bread.

* Ash-rolled goat's cheese, honey and crushed smoked almonds on rye bread.

* Tomato, red onion and chopped pickled chillies with lime juice and grilled halloumi in a flatbread.

* Thinly sliced Asiago and Parmesan-style cheese with pickled peppers, Charroux mustard and olive oil.

* Crispbread with cream cheese, rosemary salt and cherry chutney.

## BOB & JAC

* The 'retro Aussie': dried apricots soaked in orange juice, topped with cream cheese, walnut pieces and sprinkled with crushed pistachios.

* 'Mad birds toastie': toasted bread topped with ricotta, Branston pickle, sliced green apple and sesame seeds, topped with alfalfa sprouts.

* Crisp omelette: when a plain omelette is almost cooked, chuck in a handful of lightly crushed crisps.

* Sandwich cold leftover dhal between two slices of bread and toast in a toasted sandwich maker.

* Crunchy peanut butter, a pinch of salt crystals, Cheddar, sliced tomatoes and salad cream on crusty white bread.

## ADDIE

* Microwave a pain au chocolat for 20 seconds, then pour over chocolate milk and nuke for another 20 seconds. Top with sliced banana and 2 teaspoons of peanut butter.

## BETH

* Cheese and brinjal pickle in a toasted sandwich maker.

* Hot cross buns made into a toasted cheese sandwich.

* Eggy bread with smoked paprika, dipped in garlic mayo and chilli sauce.

* Olives, parsley and chopped garlic on toast, with a squeeze of lemon.

* Field mushrooms topped with Boursin, then roasted in the oven.

## GEORGIA & FAMILY

* Bread dipped in olive oil, then za'atar.

* Pickled garlic and olives.

* Popping candy sprinkled on pineapple slices.

* Chocolate bar chunks frozen in a banana.

## HENRY

* Peanut butter and avocado on toast.

* Cold baked beans eaten straight out of the tin, with added Worcestershire sauce.

## JANE

* Cook some curry-flavoured instant noodles. Take off the heat and stir in a beaten egg and chopped spring onion, red chilli and coriander.

* Grated cheese, chopped tomato and Branston pickle on toast, nuked in the oven or microwave.

## CHRISTINE

* Wafer-thin Sardinian Carta di musica (thin, crisp bread) with tomatoes, rocket and Parmesan (or any other leftovers).

## ANITA & MATT

* Diced apple, diced cheese and raisins.

* Rice cakes with maple syrup.

* Peanut butter dipped into Marmite … on way to gob.

## ABI

* Sweet potato, microwaved, then topped with salt and salad cream.

# SALADS

LEON

# Bean, Fennel & Feta Salad

SERVES 4 • PREPARATION TIME: 10 MINUTES
COOKING TIME: 5 MINUTES • ♥ ✓ WF GF V

A simple salad.

200g **French beans**, topped and tailed

1 head of **fennel**, trimmed

1 small bunch of **fresh flat-leaf parsley**, leaves removed and shredded

70g **feta cheese**, crumbled

2 tablespoons **toasted pine nuts**

**FOR THE DRESSING**

1 generous teaspoon **Dijon mustard**

50ml **lemon juice**

100ml **olive oil**

**salt** and **freshly ground black pepper**

1. Bring a large pan of salted water to the boil. Add the beans and blanch for 3–4 minutes, until tender (just past the squeaky stage). Set aside to cool.

2. Finely shred the fennel, either on a mandolin or using a sharp knife.

3. Whisk the dressing ingredients together.

4. Put the beans, fennel, parsley, feta and pine nuts into a bowl and mix together. Toss with the dressing and season well.

# Jackson Pollock Salad

SERVES 8 • PREPARATION TIME: 10 MINUTES • COOKING TIME: 35 MINUTES • ♥ WF GF DF V

A beautiful burst of colour to serve on a summer's day, on its own, or alongside a barbecue.

300g **Camargue red rice**

200g podded **broad beans**

200g **red onions**

200g soft **dried apricots**

4 tablespoons **olive oil**

juice of 1 **lemon**

**salt** and **freshly ground black pepper**

100g **pistachio nuts**

2 tablespoons chopped **fresh coriander**

JOSEPH, LIZA, HENRY & EDMUND, FRANCE 1977

I created this dish for a summer barbecue with a bunch of restaurateurs and chefs. I think it was a triumph, but Henry Harris of Racine restaurant in London produced an extraordinary and extraordinarily alcoholic trifle for pudding, and no one remembered much after that.

HENRY

1. Cook the rice in boiling salted water for 30 minutes, or until tender but still chewy. Drain well.

2. Bring a pan of salted water to the boil. Add the broad beans and cook for 1–2 minutes, until tender, then drain in a colander and refresh under cold water. Skin the larger broad beans and set aside.

3. Peel and finely slice the onions and put into a large bowl. Chop the apricots into raisin-sized pieces and add to the bowl with the rice, oil and lemon juice. Season well.

4. Just before serving, toast the pistachios for 2 minutes in a frying pan over a medium heat. Allow to cool, then crush with a rolling pin and mix into the salad.

5. Stir in the broad beans and coriander. Check the seasoning and serve.

**VARIATIONS**

✿ Instead of Camargue red rice, use wild rice, pearl barley, brown rice or spelt.

✿ Runner beans or French beans can be used in place of broad beans (or you can substitute frozen peas).

✿ Try other herbs instead of coriander – fresh mint and parsley, or strong-flavoured leaves such as rocket or mustard.

# Grilled Spring Onions, Asparagus & Courgettes

## WITH WHITE BEANS & BASIL DRESSING

SERVES 4 • PREPARATION TIME: 10 MINUTES • COOKING TIME: 15 MINUTES • ♥ ✓ WF GF DF V

Spring onions are readily available all year round, but if you can find some of the more bulbous bunched onions in May, try them instead of the usual pencil-thin sort for a change.

250g **asparagus spears**

2 bunches of **spring onions**

3 **courgettes**

1 tablespoon **olive oil**

**salt** and **freshly ground black pepper**

200g cooked **haricot/ cannellini/flageolet beans**

**FOR THE BASIL DRESSING**

1 clove of **garlic**, crushed

1 bunch of **fresh basil**, leaves picked

2 tablespoons **olive oil**

1. First, prepare the vegetables, keeping them in separate piles. Snap the woody ends off the asparagus spears. Cut off the very green ends of the spring onions, along with the roots, and peel away any tough outer skin. Top and tail the courgettes and cut them lengthways into thin sheets.

2. Heat a griddle pan. Toss each pile of vegetables in a little olive oil, then grill in batches for a few minutes on each side. Season well.

3. Make the dressing by blending the garlic, basil and olive oil together with a little salt, in a blender or using a pestle and mortar.

4. Put the veg, beans and dressing into a large bowl and toss together, then check the seasoning and serve.

## TIPS

* The basil dressing above is versatile and packs a punch. It can be used with a variety of other vegetables, especially tomatoes and grilled aubergines.

* Roasting asparagus for a few minutes in a medium/ high oven is another method of cooking this lovely vegetable and intensifying its flavour. They only need to be tossed in a little oil, pepper and salt beforehand.

# Vegetables & Tofu with Thai Dressing

SERVES 4 • PREPARATION TIME: 15 MINUTES • COOKING TIME: NONE • ♥ WF GF DF V

Don't be put off by the long ingredients list here. The secret is in the dressing, and in getting the balance of flavours right to create a wonderful, creamy sauce that works with any salad with blanched vegetables. The salad ingredients below are just a guide, not a rigid list.

### FOR THE DRESSING

100g **unsalted roasted peanuts**

125ml **lime juice**

3 tablespoons **rice vinegar**

3 cloves of **garlic**, crushed

3 tablespoons chopped **fresh coriander** (including stalks and roots)

2 tablespoons **palm sugar** (or soft brown sugar)

1 teaspoon **tamarind paste**

1 **red chilli**, chopped (optional)

3 tablespoons **water**

**salt**

### FOR THE SALAD

2 **Little Gem lettuces** or similar

100g **tofu**, cut into small cubes

1 small **cucumber**

4 **tomatoes**

1 bunch of **spring onions**, chopped

3 **hard-boiled eggs**

100g **broccoli florets**, blanched

1 **red pepper**

1. Put all the dressing ingredients into a liquidizer and blend until the mixture has the consistency of pouring cream. Taste and check the seasoning.

2. Wash the lettuces, stripping away any discoloured leaves, then wash and dry well in a salad spinner. Break the lettuce into separate leaves and arrange them on a large plate. Chop the rest of the salad ingredients into slices or chunks and scatter over the leaves, then drizzle with the dressing and serve.

**TIPS**

* The dressing is lovely tossed through some quickly stir-fried vegetables and served with rice.

* This recipe also works well as a simple topping for steamed rice or noodles.

# Little Gem & Egg Salad

## WITH ANISEED DRESSING

SERVES 4 • PREPARATION TIME: 10 MINUTES • COOKING TIME: 6 MINUTES • ♥ ✓ WF GF DF V

The dressing below involves an unusual list of ingredients, but it works very well and could be served on its own as a dip.

2–3 **Little Gem lettuces**
(depending on size)

4 **eggs**

chopped **fresh parsley**,
to serve

**FOR THE ANISEED DRESSING**

3 tablespoons **hummus**

1 tablespoon chopped
**fresh tarragon leaves**

1 tablespoon chopped
**fresh parsley**

1 **shallot**, chopped

juice of ½ a **lemon**

1 teaspoon **Dijon mustard**

2 teaspoons **soy sauce**

2 teaspoons **Pernod/anisette**

3 tablespoons **olive oil**

**salt** and **freshly ground
black pepper**

1. Wash the lettuces, stripping away any discoloured leaves, then wash and dry well in a salad spinner.

2. Boil the eggs in water for 6 minutes, then refresh in cold water and remove the shells.

3. Blend all the dressing ingredients together, using an immersion blender or a liquidizer. If the mixture is too thick to drizzle, add a little water. Season well.

4. Cut the lettuces into 8 wedges and arrange on a serving dish. Drizzle with some of the dressing.

5. Roughly chop the eggs and scatter over the lettuce, then pour over more dressing, sprinkle with parsley and serve.

**TIPS**

Optional toppings:
- Crunchy croûtons.
- Toasted almonds and pumpkin seeds.

The dressing in this recipe takes its origins from Courchamps sauce, made with the brown meat of crab or lobster. The sauce has an aniseed flavour and is generally served in salads with the white meat of these shellfish. We tried replacing the brown meat with hummus and the results were great. It is quite a rich sauce so it needs to be served with simple fare.

JANE

# Spring Vegetable & Farro Salad

SERVES 4 • PREPARATION TIME: 5 MINUTES • COOKING TIME: 40 MINUTES • ♥ DF V

If you have difficulty finding farro, pearled spelt or barley can be substituted. Frying the grain helps to enhance the nutty flavour.

200g **farro**

**salt** and **freshly ground black pepper**

150g **asparagus spears**

150g **sugar snap peas**

2 tablespoons **olive oil**

4 cloves of **garlic**, finely chopped

3 tablespoons **mixed fresh herbs** (tarragon, chives, dill), chopped

2 teaspoons good **vinegar**

1. Rinse the farro (or other grain, if using) under cold running water. Drain, then place in a pan and cover with water. Add a little salt, then bring to a simmer and cook for about 30 minutes, until the farro is tender but still has a little bite to it.

2. Drain the farro in a sieve, then rinse under cold water and set aside over a bowl to drain again.

3. While the farro is cooking, prepare the vegetables. Snap the woody ends off the asparagus and cut the spears into 2cm lengths. Top and tail the sugar snaps and slice across on the diagonal.

4. Bring a large pan of salted water to the boil. Add the asparagus and cook for 1 minute, then drain.

5. Heat the oil in a large, shallow frying pan, then add the garlic and cook over a medium heat for 1 minute. Tip in the farro, mix well and cook, stirring continuously, for 5 minutes. Season well.

6. Add the asparagus and sugar snaps and cook for another 2 minutes. Stir in the herbs and vinegar, and serve at room temperature.

**TIPS**

* Otherways with farro:
  • Combine it with tomatoes, fried courgette pieces and aubergines, then stir through a little pesto to make a salad.
  • Fry it with cooked sweetcorn and red peppers.
  • Toss it with cooked French beans, crumbled feta and chopped olives.

This is a recipe from L'Osteria del Matto in Spoleto, Umbria. I was lucky enough to eat an extraordinary meal there, cooked by the owner Filippo's mother, Santina. She is 70, and cooks a set menu in the small restaurant twice a day, in a kitchen that makes most galley kitchens look vast. Santina kindly explained how she made her farro salad (on which the above is based) and also her deep-fried ricotta, which I must never divulge – having been sworn to secrecy as to its content.

JANE

SANTINA, SPOLETO, UMBRIA, 2012

# Salvatore's Panzanella

SERVES 4–6 • PREPARATION TIME: 15 MINUTES • COOKING TIME: NONE • ♥ DF V

Panzanella is traditionally a Tuscan summer salad; however, this version comes from a Sicilian chef, cooking in Umbria. The bread used in the original version was a very dry barley roll, but a dense wholemeal or sourdough loaf makes a good substitute.

250g stale **sourdough/ wholemeal bread**, ripped into 2–3cm pieces

60ml good **red wine vinegar**

60ml **olive oil**

1 clove of **garlic**, crushed

500g **cherry** or **good-quality ripe tomatoes**

**salt** and **freshly ground black pepper**

a bunch of **fresh basil**

1 **celery heart**, thinly sliced

1 small **red onion**, thinly sliced

50g **stoned olives**

a pinch of **dried oregano**

lots of good **olive oil**

1. Put the bread into a wide, shallow serving dish. Put the vinegar, oil and garlic into a bowl and mix together, then drizzle over the bread, mixing it in well with your hands.

2. Halve the tomatoes, sprinkle with salt and add to the bread.

3. Set aside a few leaves of basil for the garnish and scatter the rest over the bread, along with the celery, onion and olives. Sprinkle with a little oregano and drizzle with lots of good olive oil.

4. Cover the dish and set to one side in a cool place until ready to serve.

## TIPS

* This is a great salad, as it can be made in advance and seems to improve with keeping.

* Panzanella can also be made with capers and roasted peppers.

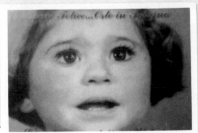
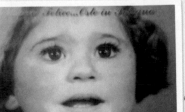

This recipe comes via a friend, Christine Smallwood (author of the book *An Appetite for Umbria*), who introduced me to its creator, Salvatore, on a recent trip to Umbria. Salvatore once ran the world-renowned restaurant Il Bacco Felice, in Foligno. As well as its superb food Il Bacco was also famous for its hospitality, which was generally down to the exuberance of its host Salvo and his ability to bring his guests together to create an unrivalled atmosphere. The 'King of Pork (and cork)', as he was known to his customers, Salvatore still has a vegetable garden where he grows a huge array of some 54 types of tomato in one year. He now cooks at the Arnaldo Caprai winery in Montefalco, Italy.

JANE

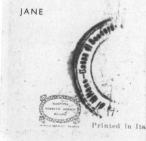

SALVATORE, AGE 2, SICILY

# Fennel, Radish & Broad Bean Salad

SERVES 4 • PREPARATION TIME: 10 MINUTES • COOKING TIME: 5 MINUTES • ♥ WF GF DF V

An easy, pretty salad with a cooked dressing.

200g podded **broad beans**

1 tablespoon **olive oil**

**salt** and **freshly ground black pepper**

1 head of **fennel**

100g **radishes**

1 bunch of **watercress**

**FOR THE DRESSING**

60g **sesame seeds**

grated zest and juice of 1 **orange**

1 clove of **garlic**, crushed

1 tablespoon **sesame oil**

1 tablespoon **balsamic vinegar**

2 teaspoons **honey**

1. Bring a pan of salted water to the boil, then add the broad beans and cook for 2 minutes, or until tender. Drain, then put into a bowl and toss in the olive oil while still hot. Season well with salt and pepper and set aside to cool.

2. Trim the fennel and cut in half lengthways. Slice across each half very thinly. Wash the radishes and slice very thinly. Add the radishes and fennel to the bowl of broad beans.

3. Dry-fry the sesame seeds in a small non-stick frying pan over a medium heat for a few minutes, until they start to brown and pop. Quickly add the orange zest and juice and the garlic and simmer until the volume has reduced by half. Remove from the heat and add the rest of the dressing ingredients. Allow to cool, then season well.

4. Add the dressing to the bowl of vegetables and toss well. Finally, gently fold in the watercress and serve.

**TIPS**

* Change the salad into a type of Middle Eastern fattoush by adding a little ground cumin to the dressing and tossing through some toasted pieces of pitta bread.

* Try cooking radishes by braising them in a little sugar, vinegar and butter.

* If the broad beans are large and tough it may be necessary to peel off their outer skins.

* Grilling the fennel slightly will add a smoky flavour.

# Aubergines, Pomegranate & Mint

## WITH A TAHINI DRESSING

SERVES 4 • PREPARATION TIME: 10 MINUTES • COOKING TIME: 10 MINUTES • ♥ ✓ WF GF DF V

Pomegranate seeds add a little sharp 'pop' to savoury dishes and are visually stunning. This dressing is also good with falafel and other vegetable fritters.

1 large **aubergine**

3 tablespoons **olive oil**

1 tablespoon good **red wine vinegar**

seeds from 1 **pomegranate**

1 tablespoon shredded **fresh mint leaves**

**FOR THE TAHINI DRESSING**

2 cloves of **garlic**, crushed

1 tablespoon **tahini**

125ml **natural yoghurt**

juice of 1 **lemon**

1 tablespoon **honey**

a pinch of **cayenne pepper**

a pinch of **ground cumin**

**salt** and **freshly ground black pepper**

1. To make the dressing, place all the ingredients in a liquidizer (or put into a bowl and use an immersion blender) and blend together, adding a little water until you have a mixture with the consistency of double cream. Season well.

2. Slice the aubergine into discs about 5mm thick.

3. Heat the oil in a shallow frying pan, then add the aubergine slices and cook over a medium heat until lightly browned on both sides. You will need to do this in batches. When each batch is ready, remove from the pan and drain on kitchen paper.

4. Arrange the aubergine slices on a large plate. Sprinkle them with the vinegar and season well. Drizzle with the tahini dressing and scatter over the pomegranate seeds and mint.

**TIPS**

* To remove the seeds from a pomegranate, cut it in half across the middle. Take one half and place it cut side down on the palm of your hand. With the other hand, bash the pomegranate half with a rolling pin, quite firmly – the seeds should just come away.

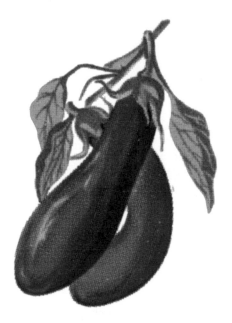

# Grilled Corn, Avocado & Toasted Tortilla Salad

SERVES 4 • PREPARATION TIME: 15 MINUTES • COOKING TIME: 20 MINUTES • ♥ WF GF V

This salad can be made with plain cooked sweetcorn, but if you grill it, the corn takes on a smoky flavour. Teamed up with the crisp tortilla strips, it makes a funky, tasty salad.

4 cobs of **sweetcorn with husks**, soaked in cold water for 10 minutes

**salt** and **freshly ground black pepper**

2 **corn tortillas**, cut into strips about 1cm wide

2 **avocados**, peeled, stoned and sliced

100g **cherry tomatoes**, halved

70g **feta cheese** (or goat's cheese), crumbled

**fresh coriander**, chopped

**fresh mint**, chopped

**FOR THE DRESSING**

1 small **red onion**, chopped

2 **green chillies**, chopped

1 tablespoon **piquillo peppers**, chopped (or any other jarred or peeled peppers)

3 tablespoons **olive oil**

juice of 1 **lime**

**salt** and **cayenne pepper**

1. Put the dressing ingredients into a wide serving bowl, mix together well and season.

2. Grill the corn on a preheated griddle pan (or on a barbecue), turning often until well browned. This should take 10–15 minutes.

3. When cool enough to handle, peel away the husks and stand the corn upright on a chopping board and cut downwards with a sawing action. Add the kernels to the bowl of dressing and season wth salt and pepper.

4. Heat the oven to 160°C/325°F/gas mark 3. Put the tortilla strips on a baking tray and put into the oven for 5–7 minutes, until crisp. Remove from the oven and let them cool, the add them to the bowl with all the other ingredients.

5. Toss well and serve immediately.

CORN WITH ITS HUSK PEELED BACK

**TIPS**

* Grilling oiled corn cobs from scratch dries them out quickly. The best way is to take corn cobs with their husks still wrapped round, blanch them until cooked, then peel back the husk, roll in oil and quickly griddle on a griddle plate to brown slightly and impart a smoky flavour.

# Grilled Carrot & Parsnip Salad

SERVES 4 • PREPARATION TIME: 10 MINUTES • COOKING TIME: 10 MINUTES • ♥ WF GF DF V

This Moroccan-style salad breathes new life into carrots and parsnips during the winter months. Chopping all your vegetables to roughly the same size will help in controlling the cooking time.

400g **carrots**

400g **parsnips**

1 tablespoon **olive oil**

**salt** and **freshly ground black pepper**

85g **watercress**

150g cooked **Puy lentils**

**FOR THE DRESSING**

2 tablespoons **olive oil**

a pinch of **ground cumin**

a pinch of **ground cinnamon**

1 tablespoon **maple syrup**

grated zest and juice of ½ an **orange**

2 **dried figs**, finely chopped

a pinch of **cayenne pepper**

1. Peel the carrots and parsnips. Place them in a pan, cover with salted water and bring to the boil. Reduce the heat and simmer for 3 minutes, then drain and allow to cool.

2. Slice the vegetables lengthways into strips 3–5mm thick. Put into a bowl, toss with the olive oil and season well.

3. Whisk together the dressing ingredients and pour into a shallow bowl.

4. Heat a griddle plate or pan and grill the vegetable strips in batches so that they have charred ridges on each side. As each batch is ready, remove it from the griddle and toss in the dressing while still hot. Allow to cool.

5. Just before serving, add the watercress and lentils to the vegetables and gently fold in. Arrange on a serving dish and serve.

**TIPS**

* Seasoned yoghurt, feta, goat's cheese or Tahini Dressing (see page 81) sprinkled over are all alternative ways to finish off this dish.

# FRITTERS
# & PANCAKES

LEON

# Kale & Feta Spiced Fritters

SERVES 4 • PREPARATION TIME: 10 MINUTES • COOKING TIME: 10 MINUTES • WF GF V

Henry first knocked these up using leftovers he found in his fridge for a Monday night supper.

250g **kale**

100g **gram flour**

1 teaspoon **ground cumin**

1 teaspoon **ground paprika**

½ teaspoon **ground turmeric**

**salt** and **freshly ground black pepper**

150ml **milk**

75g **feta cheese**, crumbled

2 tablespoons **olive oil**

1. Wash the kale and strip away the leaves from the central rib. Bring a large pan of salted water to the boil and cook the leaves for 2 minutes, until tender, then drain and refresh under cold running water. Squeeze out excess moisture and chop the leaves roughly.

2. Sift the gram flour, spices and a pinch of salt into a large bowl. Add the milk slowly, beating to make a thick batter. Stir in the crumbled feta, followed by the chopped kale. Season the mixture well.

3. Heat the oil in a non-stick frying pan and drop in tablespoons of the batter to make small fritters. Cook for a few minutes on each side and serve.

**TIPS**

* This is good served with the Tomato & Ginger Chutney (see below) or try a fresh tomato salsa.

* We use cavolo nero here, but it is equally good with curly or red Russian kale.

* Try substituting blue cheese or goat's cheese for the feta.

# Fresh Tomato & Ginger Chutney

MAKES 500ML • PREPARATION TIME: 10 MINUTES • COOKING TIME: 7 MINUTES • ♥ WF GF DF V

This is a fresh chutney that's very quick to make. It would be good served with a spicy main dish or as an alternative to ketchup.

120g **fresh ginger**

60ml **olive oil**

800g whole **cherry tomatoes**

**salt** and **freshly ground black pepper**

1. Peel the ginger and cut into fine julienne strips. Heat the oil in a large pan, add the ginger, and cook for 2 minutes over a medium heat.

2. Add the tomatoes, season well and let them soften for 5 minutes in the ginger oil.

3. Serve warm or cold. Keep in the fridge for up to 1 week.

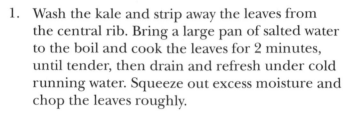

I use this method for cooking tomatoes a lot. Just knocking the edges of them with a quick blast of heat and countering the tomato's acid with some oil, yoghurt or butter. With garlic, onion, butter and a handful of fresh herbs it makes a great pasta sauce. Or try cooking meatballs and then throwing the toms into the heated pan followed by yoghurt and herbs for a quick sauce. HENRY

# Stuffed Chillies

SERVES 4 • PREPARATION TIME: 20 MINUTES • COOKING TIME: 30 MINUTES • WF GF V

These chillies can be fried, either coated in a batter or covered with crushed tortilla chips as they are in the recipe below. However, here we are going to bake them in the oven, as this is easier for most people (and healthier). The poblano chillies used below are large and fairly mild, but don't let that stop you applying the same recipe to a smaller, stronger variety.

1 **red onion**, finely diced

3 teaspoons **balsamic vinegar**

2 teaspoons **honey**

**salt** and **freshly ground black pepper**

8 **poblano chillies** (or small peppers)

1 tablespoon **olive oil**

2 tablespoons chopped **fresh mint**

2 tablespoons chopped **fresh coriander**

1 clove of **garlic**, crushed

75g **Gruyère cheese**, grated

75g **feta cheese**, crumbled

150g cooked **sweetcorn kernels**

100g **gram flour**

3 **egg whites**

100g **tortilla chips**, crushed

**olive oil**, for brushing

1. Preheat the oven to 220°C/425°F/gas mark 7.

2. Put the diced onion into a bowl with the balsamic vinegar, honey and a little salt and set aside to marinate.

3. Put the chillies into a bowl and toss with the olive oil. Place them on a baking tray and pop them into the oven for about 10 minutes, until the skin has started to blister. Remove from the oven, place in a bowl, cover tightly with clingfilm and leave until cool enough to handle. Turn the oven down to 180°C/350°F/gas mark 4.

4. Peel away the skin from the chillies, being careful to keep them intact.

5. Put the chopped herbs and garlic into a bowl and add the cheeses and the sweetcorn kernels. Stir in the marinated onions and season well. Make a slit in each chilli and remove the seeds, then stuff them with the herb mixture.

6. Get ready three shallow bowls. Put the gram flour into the first, lightly whisk the egg whites in the second, and put the crushed tortilla chips into the third. To coat the chillies, dip each one first into the flour, then into the egg white and finally into the crushed tortilla chips.

7. Place on a baking tray, brush (or spray) with olive oil, and bake in the oven for 20 minutes, or until golden.

**TIPS**

* Good with a fresh tomato salsa.

* The filling used for the chillies can be used to make quesadillas: use corn tortillas, add a spoonful of filling, then roll them up and fry them in butter on both sides. Alternatively, try it between two slices of bread as a toasted sandwich.

* Crushed tortilla chips make a great wheat-free alternative for any dish that requires a breadcrumb coating.

# Deep-fried Pickled Mushrooms

SERVES 4 • PREPARATION TIME: 10 MINUTES • COOKING TIME: 15 MINUTES • ♥ DF V

The pickling of the mushrooms can be done days before frying them, and the longer you leave them in the pickling liquor, the tastier they will be. Any mushrooms can be used – good-quality chestnut or field mushrooms work well, as do shiitake.

125ml **rice vinegar**

3 tablespoons **maple syrup**

2 tablespoons **light soy sauce**

1 slice of **fresh ginger**

1 teaspoon **dried chilli flakes**

300g **mushrooms**

**sunflower oil**, for deep-frying

100g **plain flour**

2 **eggs**

100g **dried breadcrumbs** (Japanese panko crumbs work well)

1. Put the vinegar, maple syrup, soy sauce, ginger and chilli flakes into a pan and bring to a simmer. Tip in the mushrooms and stir. At this point it will not look as though there is enough liquid to cover the mushrooms, but as they cook they will give out lots of juice.

2. Simmer the mushrooms for 10 minutes, then remove from the heat and allow to cool in the pickling liquor. At this point the mushrooms and their liquid can be kept in a sterilized jar in the fridge for up to 2 weeks.

3. To make the mushroom fritters, heat the sunflower oil to 180°C in a deep-fat fryer or large pan. Remove the mushrooms from their liquid and pat dry with kitchen paper.

4. Get ready three shallow bowls. Put the flour into the first, beat the eggs in the second, and put the breadcrumbs into the third. Toss the mushrooms in the flour, then dip them into the beaten egg, and finally roll them in breadcrumbs.

5. Deep-fry the mushrooms for a few minutes, or until golden brown. Drain on kitchen paper before serving.

JANE AND HER BROTHER JOHN AT HOME IN SUNDERLAND, 1974

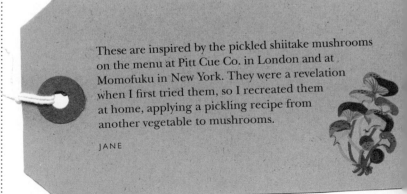

These are inspired by the pickled shiitake mushrooms on the menu at Pitt Cue Co. in London and at Momofuku in New York. They were a revelation when I first tried them, so I recreated them at home, applying a pickling recipe from another vegetable to mushrooms.

JANE

# Rosie's Pea, Mint & Sharpham Rustic Fritters

MAKES 6 FRITTERS (ENOUGH FOR 4–6) • PREPARATION TIME: 5 MINUTES • COOKING TIME: 10 MINUTES • V

The cheese used is from Sharpham estate, from where the recipe originates, but any semi-soft cheese can be used instead (or even diced halloumi). Frozen peas are fine to use here.

500g **peas**

230ml **milk**

4 **eggs**

60g **cornflour**

200g **self-raising flour**

1 teaspoon **baking powder**

200g **Sharpham Rustic cheese**, cut into small cubes

**salt** and **freshly ground black pepper**

**olive oil**, for frying

1. Bring a pan of salted water to the boil, add the peas and cook for 2 minutes, then drain and crush roughly with a potato masher.

2. Whisk the milk and eggs together in a bowl. Sift the flours and baking powder and add to the egg mixture, whisking to form a batter.

3. Add the crushed peas and the cheese, season well and stir to combine.

4. Heat a little oil in a non-stick pan. Drop in the mixture a dessertspoon at a time, flatten slightly, and fry the patties gently until browned on both sides. Drain on kitchen paper.

ROSIE ON DARTMOOR, AGED 3

**T I P S**

* Serve with a fresh tomato salsa or Mint Yoghurt Sauce (see page 129).

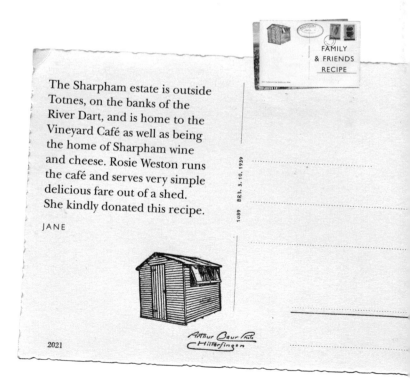

FAMILY & FRIENDS RECIPE

The Sharpham estate is outside Totnes, on the banks of the River Dart, and is home to the Vineyard Café as well as being the home of Sharpham wine and cheese. Rosie Weston runs the café and serves very simple delicious fare out of a shed. She kindly donated this recipe.

JANE

2021

# Potato Pancakes with Beetroot Salad

MAKES ABOUT 20 (ENOUGH FOR 4–6) • PREPARATION TIME: 15 MINUTES • COOKING TIME: 15 MINUTES • WF GF V

These little pancakes puff up beautifully and melt in the mouth. They are best eaten hot, straight off the griddle. However, you can reheat them, so it is worth cooking a large batch as they are so versatile. Children love them.

**FOR THE POTATO PANCAKES**

350g warm **mashed potato**

50g **rice flour**

50g **gram flour**

2 **eggs**

2 **egg yolks**

100ml **milk**

1 heaped tablespoon **crème fraîche**

a pinch of **bicarbonate of soda**

a pinch of **cayenne pepper**

**salt** and **freshly ground black pepper**

1 tablespoon **olive oil**

**FOR THE BEETROOT SALAD**

300g **raw beetroot**

1 tablespoon **olive oil**

2 teaspoons **caraway seeds**

1 clove of **garlic**, crushed

5 tablespoons **orange juice**

1 teaspoon **sugar**

2 tablespoons **crème fraîche**

1 tablespoon grated **horseradish**

1 tablespoon chopped **fresh chives**

1. Put the mashed potato and both flours into a bowl and mix together, then beat in the eggs and egg yolks. Add the milk and crème fraîche and whip together, adding the bicarbonate of soda and cayenne. Season well.

2. Heat the oil in a non-stick frying pan. Drop large tablespoons of the batter into the pan and cook for 2–3 minutes on each side, until golden. You will need to cook the pancakes in batches. Keep them warm until ready to serve.

3. To make the salad, peel and grate the beetroots using a coarse grater or a food processor. Season.

4. Heat the oil in a frying pan. Add the caraway seeds and cook for a few minutes, then add the garlic, orange juice and sugar and bring to the boil. Lower the heat and simmer until reduced to half the volume – the mixture should have a syrupy consistency. Tip in the beetroot and stir to ensure it is well coated. Season.

5. Put the crème fraîche into a bowl and stir in the grated horseradish.

6. To serve, pile up the beetroot on top of the pancakes. Top with the horseradish cream and sprinkle with some chopped chives, then serve.

**TIPS**

* These pancakes are good for serving at parties – try topping with a slice of fried smoked tofu, a blob of beetroot salad and a little of the horseradish cream.

* Using an electric hand whisk will result in a smooth batter – just don't end up wearing it.

* The beetroot salad is good enough to eat on its own or as a side – it can be tarted up with fresh orange segments. The addition of grated carrot gives it an amazing Barbie-pink colour.

# Turnip Pancakes

MAKES 10 PANCAKES (ENOUGH FOR 4–6) • PREPARATION TIME: 10 MINUTES •
COOKING TIME: 20 MINUTES • ♥ ✓ WF GF DF V

These pancakes are a cross between the Chinese yum cha version and Korean chive pancakes. Good as a starter, main or party food.

300g **turnips**

2cm piece of **fresh ginger,** grated

300ml **water**

150g **rice flour**

1 teaspoon **gram flour**

2 teaspoon **sesame seeds**

1 bunch of **spring onions**, chopped, plus extra to garnish

1 tablespoon **sesame oil**

a pinch of **cayenne pepper**

2 **red chillies**, finely chopped

1 clove of **garlic**, crushed

**salt**

2 tablespoons chopped **fresh coriander**

2–3 tablespoons **sunflower oil**, for frying

1. Peel and grate the turnips. Place in a pan with the grated ginger and the water and bring to the boil. Reduce the heat and simmer for 10 minutes, then drain, reserving the cooking liquid. Set aside and leave to cool until tepid.

2. Place the rest of the ingredients apart from the sunflower oil in a bowl and slowly add the reserved cooking liquid, whisking until a smooth batter is formed – it should have the consistency of double cream. Add the grated turnip and check the seasoning.

3. Heat 1 tablespoon of sunflower oil in a non-stick frying pan and drop in the batter a dessertspoon at a time, to form small round pancakes – flatten them a little with the back of a spoon.

4. Cook for a few minutes on each side until golden, then serve sprinkled with extra spring onions.

**TIPS**

* These are great served with a soy, fresh ginger and chilli dipping sauce.

# Beetroot Rösti

## WITH HALLOUMI & SPINACH

MAKES 4 RÖSTI (ENOUGH FOR 4) • PREPARATION TIME: 10 MINUTES • COOKING TIME: 15 MINUTES • ✓ WF GF V

Röstis are usually made using potatoes, but you can use any root vegetable. The beetroot used here makes purple fritters, which form a good base for a variety of toppings or can be eaten alone as a quick, simple snack.

400g **raw beetroots**, peeled and grated

1 **onion**, finely chopped

1 tablespoon **gram flour**

1 **egg**

1 tablespoon **olive oil**

150g **spinach**, washed

**salt** and **freshly ground black pepper**

100g **halloumi cheese**

30g **butter**

12 **fresh sage leaves**

1. Heat the oven to 180°C/350°F/gas mark 4.

2. Place the grated beetroot and chopped onion in a tea towel and squeeze out any excess moisture.

3. Put the gram flour into a bowl. Whisk the egg and mix into the flour, seasoning well. Stir in the beetroot and onion.

4. Heat the olive oil in a non-stick frying pan. Add a quarter of the mixture, flattening it into a disc with a wooden spoon, and fry on one side for 2 minutes over a medium heat. Flip over and cook the other side for 2 minutes, then slide it on to a baking tray and put it straight into the oven and bake for 5 minutes. Repeat with the rest of the mixture to make three more rösti.

5. Heat a large pan over a high heat. Tip in the washed spinach, stir quickly and season, then cover and leave to wilt for a minute. Remove from the heat and keep warm.

6. Cut the halloumi into 8 slices. Heat a non-stick pan and fry the cheese slices for 1 minute on each side.

7. Melt the butter in a small pan and add the sage leaves. Allow the butter to froth, then remove the sage leaves when crispy.

8. To serve, place a rösti on each plate and top with the spinach, halloumi and crispy sage leaves.

**TIPS**

* Caraway seeds can be added to the rösti mix with the flour.

* The dish can be finished with a sprinkling of toasted nuts.

# Vegetable Fritto Misto

SERVES 4 • PREPARATION TIME: 10 MINUTES, PLUS RESTING • COOKING TIME: 5 MINUTES • ♥ V

We have provided recipes for two batters, each different, but both equally good. The second batter is the fritto batter that Mitch and Matt use at The Seahorse restaurant in Dartmouth – it is the quickest to make, but uses milk, so we have included the other method for a dairy-free alternative. The vegetables below are examples of what can be used, but most vegetables can be cooked this way if prepared correctly.

## Batter 1

150g **plain flour**

2 tablespoons **olive oil**

2 **egg whites**

**salt** and **freshly ground black pepper**

1. Sift the flour into a large bowl. Whisk in the olive oil, followed by enough lukewarm water to give the batter the consistency of double cream. Set aside for 30 minutes.

2. Whisk the egg whites until just holding their shape. Fold into the batter carefully. Season well.

**YOU WILL ALSO NEED**

**sunflower oil**, for deep-frying

**VEGETABLES (FOR USE WITH EITHER BATTER)**

**artichokes**, peeled back and cut into wedges

**aubergines**, cut across into thin rounds

**broccoli**, separated into florets

**cauliflower**, separated into florets

**courgettes**, cut in half lengthways and then into thin batons

**fennel**, cut in half lengthways and then into thin wedges

**TO FINISH**

2 tablespoons **capers**

20 **fresh sage leaves**

1 **lemon**, cut into wedges

## Batter 2

200g **'00' pasta flour**

100–200ml **milk**

**salt** and **freshly ground black pepper**

1. Sift the pasta flour into a bowl. Gradually add milk until you have a batter the consistency of double cream that will just cling to the veg. Season.

1. Take your selection of prepared vegetables and dip a few at a time into whichever batter you are using.

2. Heat the sunflower oil to 190°C in a deep-fat fryer or in a large pan and deep-fry the vegetables for a few minutes, or until golden brown. Transfer to kitchen paper to drain.

3. When all the vegetables have been cooked, throw the capers and sage leaves into the oil for a few seconds and scoop them out quickly with a slotted spoon.

4. Arrange the fried vegetables on a serving dish, sprinkle with the fried capers, sage and salt, and surround with lemon wedges for squeezing over. Serve immediately.

# Leah's Nettle Burgers

SERVES 4 • PREPARATION TIME: 20 MINUTES
COOKING TIME: 10 MINUTES • ♥ ✓ v

This is a seasonal recipe, and the two plants needed will
be at their best in mid to late spring.

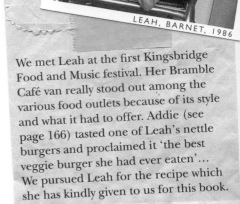

LEAH, BARNET, 1986

We met Leah at the first Kingsbridge
Food and Music festival. Her Bramble
Café van really stood out among the
various food outlets because of its style
and what it had to offer. Addie (see
page 166) tasted one of Leah's nettle
burgers and proclaimed it 'the best
veggie burger she had ever eaten'…
We pursued Leah for the recipe which
she has kindly given to us for this book.

## YOU WILL NEED:

nettles
Jack-by-the-hedge
chickpeas
kidney beans
butter
garlic
spring onions
soy sauce
cumin
ginger
honey
tahini
salt and freshly ground black pepper
oatmeal/soya protein
egg
breadcrumbs
olive oil
wholemeal seedy buns

Go for a walk and look out for a good nettle patch, preferably away from the road, and pick loads as they will shrink down when steaming. Also 'Jack-by-the-hedge', which you will find by the hedge along many banks. If you are unsure of this one then look it up – it has a garlic mustard flavour. Pick mostly the heads of both plants and then bulk it out with leaves from the top of the plants.

Open a tin of chickpeas, or soak and boil the equivalent of dried ones. If using a tin, put the chickpeas into a colander and rinse really well to get rid of the strange flavour they acquire while sitting inside a tin. Add half that amount of kidney beans.

Wash the nettles and drain them, then steam in a saucepan with a lid, using only the water left on them from washing. After a minute they should have wilted. Add a knob of butter and a handful of chopped garlic. Mash the chickpeas with the nettles, then chop the Jack-by-the-hedge and add that to the mixture raw. Then put a bunch of chopped spring onions into the mix.

Add a few teaspoons of soy sauce and 3 more cloves of garlic, 2 heaped teaspoons of ground cumin and some fresh ginger, a generous teaspoon of honey and tahini, adjusting to suit your own taste. Generously season with sea salt and black pepper.

Add either some oatmeal or textured soya protein and an egg to the mix and bind everything together. Keep adding the oatmeal until you get the right consistency for making into burgers.

Once you have reached a happy consistency, shape the mixture into burgers of the right size to fit your buns. Leave them in the fridge overnight so that they set and hold together better.

Lightly coat the burgers with breadcrumbs and fry them on a high heat in olive oil until golden brown.

Find some lovely wholegrain seedy buns – I recommend serving these burgers with a yoghurt sauce (see below), a bit of chilli jam and some fresh leaves.

I make a yoghurt sauce by finely chopping garlic and lightly frying it with olive oil for 30 seconds. Add a few pinches of ground cumin and turmeric, then take off the heat. Add some finely chopped Jack-by-the-hedge or fresh coriander, then the required amount of Greek yoghurt. Stir, and there you have a tasty garlicky yellowish yoghurt sauce.

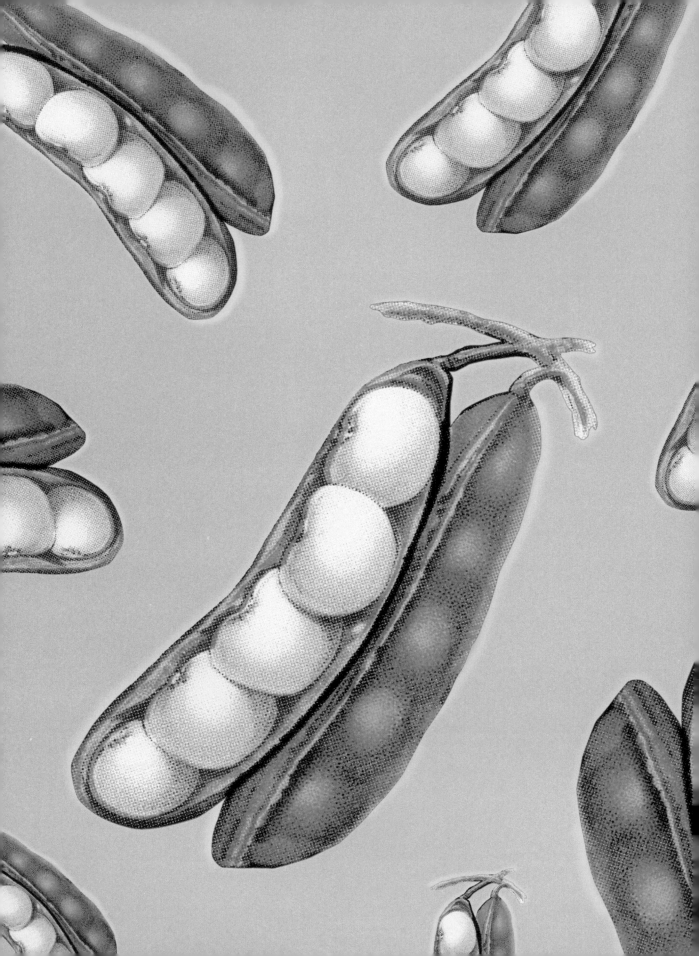

# PASTA, GRAINS & PULSES

LEON

# Orecchiette

## WITH PEAS & SPINACH

SERVES 4 • PREPARATION TIME: 10 MINUTES • COOKING TIME: 15 MINUTES • ♥ DF V

The traditional pasta of Puglia, this is generally made with *cima de rapa*, anchovies, chilli and garlic. Orecchiette means 'little ears' in Italian. This dish is a little more accessible ingredients-wise, but still has the basic flavours (anchovies can be added with the peas).

150ml **white wine**

2 cloves of **garlic**, crushed

2 **red chillies**, deseeded and chopped

300g **peas** (frozen are fine)

150ml **water**

100g **spinach**, washed

**salt** and **freshly ground black pepper**

440g **orecchiette**

2 tablespoons chopped **fresh flat-leaf parsley**

good **extra virgin olive oil**, for drizzling

1. Put the wine, garlic and chillies into a large pan and bring to the boil, then reduce the heat to medium and simmer until the volume has reduced by half.

2. Add the peas to the pan with the water and simmer for 2 minutes.

3. Next add the spinach and stir quickly to wilt, then remove from the heat.

4. Remove half the pea/spinach mix from the pan and blitz in a blender or food processor, then return it to the pan, stir and season well.

5. Bring a large pan of salted water to the boil. Add the pasta and cook for about 10–12 minutes (or according to the instructions on the packet), then drain.

6. Toss the pasta with the sauce, add the parsley and mix well. Season, and serve drizzled with good olive oil.

**TIPS**

* See the guide on how to make Fresh Orecchiette on page 144.

* Creamed Kale (see page 234) is lovely stirred through the cooked pasta.

**VARIATIONS**

✿ Chopped, cooked chard or other greens can be substituted for the spinach.

✿ You can use broad beans instead of peas.

# Warm Soba Noodle Vegetable Salad

Here's something you can do with peanut butter other than spreading it on toast. The vegetables used can vary with the seasons. We used broccoli and cabbage.

1 x 250g packet of **wheat-free soba noodles**

300g **broccoli florets**

½ a **Savoy cabbage**, cored and shredded

### FOR THE DRESSING

120g smooth **peanut butter**

1 tablespoon **soy sauce**

2 tablespoons **warm water**

2 tablespoons **grated fresh ginger**

1 clove of **garlic**, crushed

2 tablespoons **sesame oil**

2 tablespoons **rice vinegar**

2 teaspoons **honey**

**salt** and **freshly ground black pepper**

1. Blend all the dressing ingredients together in a food processor or in a bowl using an immersion blender. Season.

2. Bring a large pan of salted water to the boil. Add the soba noodles and cook for about 9 minutes, until almost ready, then tip in the vegetables and cook for another 2 minutes. Drain, then transfer to a serving bowl and toss with the dressing while still hot. Serve.

### TIPS

* Try this with a mixture of the following: cauliflower, French and runner beans, sugar snap peas or grated root veg.

* This dressing also makes a good dip for grilled vegetable brochettes and kebabs.

# Pearl Barley Risotto

## WITH DRIED MUSHROOMS & SUGAR SNAP PEAS

SERVES 4 • PREPARATION TIME: 5 MINUTES, PLUS SOAKING • COOKING TIME: 45 MINUTES • WF GF V

A favourite simple supper.

30g **dried mushrooms**
(such as porcini)

750ml **boiling water**

1 tablespoon **olive oil**

1 **onion**, chopped

1 **leek**, chopped

200g **pearl barley**,
washed and drained

**salt** and **freshly ground
black pepper**

juice of ½ a **lemon**

200ml **white wine**

a sprig of **fresh rosemary**

150g **sugar snap peas**,
trimmed and cut diagonally
into strips

a knob of **butter** (optional)

25g **vegetarian Parmesan-style
cheese**, grated

1 tablespoon chopped
**fresh flat-leaf parsley**

1. Put the mushrooms into a bowl and pour over the boiling water. Leave to soak for 20 minutes.

2. Heat the oil in a large pan, then add the onion and leek and cook over a medium heat for 10 minutes, or until soft.

3. Strain the mushrooms, reserving the soaking liquid, and chop finely. Add to the vegetables along with the pearl barley, then turn up the heat, season well and cook for 2 minutes, stirring frequently.

4. Add the lemon juice, white wine and rosemary sprig to the pan, season well, stir and allow to simmer for 5 minutes. Now start to add the mushroom liquid about a ladleful at a time. Turn the heat down but make sure the mixture is simmering gently at all times. Keep stirring occasionally and adding mushroom liquid, so that the mixture does not stick to the pan. If you run out of mushroom liquid, use boiling water.

5. When the barley is cooked but still has a chewy texture (about 20 minutes), add the sugar snaps, butter and half the Parmesan. Remove from the heat and allow to stand for 5 minutes, then season well and serve with the remaining Parmesan sprinkled over.

# Squash Risotto

SERVES 4 • PREPARATION TIME: 10 MINUTES • COOKING TIME: 45 MINUTES • WF GF V

Make a little more than you need of this risotto so that the leftovers can be turned into the yummy arancini, or fried risotto balls (see Using Leftovers, page 20). For the best results, make a stock using the pith and seeds of the squash (see Tips, below).

500–600g **butternut squash**

1 tablespoon **olive oil**

**salt** and **freshly ground black pepper**

2 tablespoons **butter**

1 **onion**, chopped

1 **leek** (white part only), finely chopped

1 clove of **garlic**, crushed

10 **fresh sage leaves**, chopped

300g **risotto rice**

100ml **white wine** or **vermouth**

1 litre **hot vegetable stock**

1 tablespoon grated **vegetarian Parmesan-style cheese**

**TIPS**

* Garnish the risotto with some crisp fried sage leaves and a sprinkle of grated nutmeg.

* For the best colour and flavour, use the discarded insides of the squash, (i.e. the pith and seeds) to make your stock. Place these in a pan with your usual stock vegetables and seasonings (see page 23). Cover with water and simmer for 30 minutes, then strain the stock and use it to make the risotto.

1. Heat the oven to 200°C/400°F/gas mark 6. Cut the squash in half lengthways and remove the seeds and pith. Place on a baking tray, drizzle with the oil, season and put into the oven for about 20 minutes, or until just tender. Set aside.

2. Melt 1 tablespoon of butter in a large pan and add the onion, leek, garlic and sage. Cook over a medium heat for 5 minutes, stirring to make sure the vegetables don't brown.

3. Add your risotto rice and season well. Turn up the heat and stir vigorously, then add the wine and mix well.

4. Scoop out the baked squash flesh from the halves and chop it finely. Discard the skin. Add half the chopped squash to the rice mixture and set the rest aside.

5. Now, with the rice over a medium heat, start to add the hot stock a ladle at a time, stirring occasionally. After 15 minutes, the rice should be almost cooked. (If all the stock has been absorbed and the rice isn't cooked yet, add some hot water.)

6. At this point, add the remaining chopped squash to the rice. Season again, then remove from the heat and stir in the Parmesan. To make the risotto extra luxurious, the remaining tablespoon of butter can be stirred in at the end.

❀ **Saffron (risotto Milanese)**: Infuse saffron in the simmering stock, then cook finely diced onions and leeks in butter for 10 minutes. Add crushed garlic and risotto rice. Turn up the heat and stir vigorously for 2 minutes, then season and deglaze with a splash of white wine or vermouth. Start adding the saffron stock and continue until the rice is cooked. Finish with butter and vegetarian Parmesan-style cheese.

❀ **Primavera**: Add spring vegetables (asparagus, broad beans, peas, spinach) to a plain risotto 5 minutes before it is ready and finish with lots of fresh herbs.

❀ **Porcini & mushroom**: Soak dried porcini in lots of boiling water for 30 minutes. Drain, reserving the soaking liquor, then chop the porcini finely along with some fresh mushrooms. Cook with the onions and rice and use the soaking liquor for stock.

❀ **Jerusalem artichoke or cauliflower or fennel**: Cut the vegetables into small dice and cook with the onions before adding the rice, allowing the vegetables to cook with the rice in the stock.

❀ **Risi e bisi:** A simple risotto of rice and peas that is generally quite wet and very comforting.

❀ **Radicchio & Gorgonzola**: Cook the rice in red wine, with the shredded radicchio added towards the end of cooking and the crumbled cheese stirred in before serving.

# Mitch Tonks's Potato Gnocchi

## WITH TRUFFLE & PARMESAN-STYLE CHEESE

SERVES 4 • PREPARATION TIME: 20 MINUTES • COOKING TIME: 20 MINUTES • V Ⓥ

If you have fresh truffles, wonderful, but if not, you can buy very good truffle pastes these days. Failing that, some finely chopped black field mushrooms plus a little truffle oil make for a fine experience. This dish is about cream, truffles and cheese, which together are an absolute joy. Gnocchi are easy to make, no real fuss, and can be paired with a whole host of things (see our alternatives below). Gnocchi making is a skill worth practising.

600g **floury potatoes**

2 **eggs**

100g **'00' pasta flour**

**FOR THE SAUCE**

150ml **double cream**

2 tablespoons **truffle paste**

30g **vegetarian Parmesan-style cheese**, grated

**salt** and **freshly ground black pepper**

**TIPS**

* The gnocchi dough is very soft and can be quite hard to handle (because of this, it gives an amazing fluffy dumpling). If you are struggling, don't try and mark the gnocchi with a fork, just get it straight into the pan of boiling water.

* You can buy small wooden ridged boards to make the gnocchi marks.

* Alternative serving ideas:
  • Tomato sauce (see page 145).
  • Braised kale, Parmesan-style cheese & truffle oil.
  • Sautéed courgette strips, saffron & pine nuts.
  • Blue cheese, spinach & walnuts.

1. Bring a large pan of salted water to the boil and add the potatoes, still in their skins. Cook for 15 minutes, or until tender, then drain and leave until cool enough to handle. Remove the skins.

2. Pass the potatoes through a potato ricer or the fine blade of a mouli-légumes and put into a bowl. Make a well in the centre and add the eggs and flour. Mix together with your fingers to make a smooth dough.

3. Roll out into lengths the diameter of your thumb and cut across at 2cm intervals. Mark the gnocchi by rolling them over an upturned fork to make grooves (this increases the surface area for the sauce to stick to).

4. To make the sauce, put the cream, truffle paste and Parmesan into a large pan and simmer together for 2 minutes.

5. Bring a large pan of salted water to the boil and drop in the gnocchi. Cook until they float to the top, then scoop them out and put them straight into the pan of truffle sauce. The sauce should coat the gnocchi. Season and serve.

MITCH, AGE 4,
WESTON-SUPER-MARE
Proprietà artistica riservata

Every year, Mitch invites a load of cooks, pals and other characters from the food world to accompany him on a trip to Piedmont for the truffle season. A certain amount of stamina is required to get through the three days, which include copious amounts of extraordinary food and drink. (The trip was described as a 'marine-style endurance test' by one participant.) It was on one of these trips in 2011 that Henry approached me about helping him with this book after a few choice glasses of red. We had to include a truffle recipe from Mr Tonks to remind us all of very happy times in this part of Italy.

JANE

PASTA E FAGIOLI

PURPLE SPROUTING BROCCOLI FARROTTO

# Pasta e Fagioli

Pasta e fagioli (pictured on page 120) is halfway between a pasta and a soup. It should be very saucy, but not so much so that the pasta is swimming in sauce. The original recipe uses pancetta – to get a similar smoky flavour add a little smoked salt or paprika.

200g **penne**

1 tablespoon **olive oil**, plus a little for the pasta

1 **onion**, chopped

1 large **carrot**, peeled and chopped

1 **leek**, chopped

3 sticks of **celery**, chopped

3 cloves of **garlic**, crushed

1 teaspoon **dried chilli flakes**

2 teaspoons chopped **fresh rosemary**

1 x 440g tin of **chopped tomatoes**

**salt** and **freshly ground black pepper**

1 x 400g tin of **borlotti beans**, drained

100ml **vegetable stock** or **water**

**extra virgin olive oil**, to serve

**grated vegetarian Parmesan-style cheese**, to serve

1. Bring a large pan of salted water to the boil, then add the penne and cook according to the packet instructions (about 10–12 minutes), until al dente. Drain, then return to the pan and toss with a little olive oil.

2. While the pasta is cooking, heat 1 tablespoon of oil in a large pan, then add the vegetables and cook over a medium heat for 10 minutes without colouring.

3. Add the garlic, chilli flakes and rosemary and cook for 2 minutes over a low heat. Tip in the tomatoes, then turn up the heat and simmer for another 10 minutes. Season well.

4. Stir in the borlotti beans and bring to the boil, then turn off the heat.

5. Remove one-third of the mixture and put it into a blender or food processor with the stock or water. Blend until smooth, then stir it back into the mixture in the pan.

6. Tip in the cooked pasta and stir well. Bring back to a simmer, season and serve drizzled with extra virgin olive oil, and sprinkled with Parmesan.

**TIPS**

* Traditionally penne is added to this dish, although there is no reason why other pasta types can't be used. Tiny pasta shapes like digitali or orzo could be used as well as macaroni.

* You can achieve your desired 'soupiness' by altering the amount of water or vegetable stock that you add.

# Purple Sprouting Broccoli Farrotto

SERVES 4 • PREPARATION TIME: 5 MINUTES • COOKING TIME: 30 MINUTES • WF V

This is another way of using farro, cooking it in the style of risotto (pictured on page 121). Purple sprouting broccoli is widely available in the winter months and is terribly under-used. Semi-pearled farro is a good grain to use for added creaminess.

2 tablespoons **olive oil**

1 **onion**, chopped

3 cloves of **garlic**, crushed

a pinch of **dried chilli flakes**

200g **semi-pearled farro**

**salt** and **freshly ground black pepper**

300g **purple sprouting broccoli**, roughly chopped

1 litre **hot vegetable stock**

1 tablespoon **grated vegetarian Parmesan-style cheese**, to serve

**extra virgin olive oil**, to serve

1. Heat the olive oil in a large pan, add the onion and cook for 5 minutes, until soft but without colouring. Add the garlic and chilli flakes and stir.

2. Wash the farro well under running cold water and drain. Add to the onion and turn up the heat, stirring so that it doesn't stick to the pan. Season.

3. Tip in the chopped broccoli, mix well and turn the heat down. Cook together for a minute, then add a little stock, just enough to cover the farro, and bring to a simmer. Slowly add the rest of the stock as you would for a risotto, stirring well between additions and cooking for a few minutes before adding the next ladleful.

4. When the farro is tender, remove from the heat (if you run out of stock, use a little hot water) and allow to stand. Stir in grated Parmesan to taste, drizzle with extra virgin olive oil and serve.

**TIPS**

* Try adding roughly chopped spinach or chard right at the end of cooking with a knob of butter and some freshly grated nutmeg.

**VARIATIONS**

✿ Farro can be used in place of rice in most risotto recipes.

✿ A combination of the purple sprouting and black kale makes a great combination.

# Quinoa Salad

The dressed cooked quinoa is lovely to eat on its own, as well as with the additions listed in the recipe. In fact, all kinds of vegetables, nuts, and other ingredients can be added to make a great salad (see the suggestions in the Tips below).

200g **quinoa**

1 tablespoon **olive oil**

500ml **water**

**FOR THE DRESSING**

juice of 1 **lime**

1 tablespoon **rice vinegar**

1 tablespoon **maple syrup**

1 **red chilli**, chopped

1 **red onion**, finely chopped

1 clove of **garlic**, crushed

**salt** and **freshly ground black pepper**

**OUR SUGGESTED ADDITIONS**

10 **cherry tomatoes**, cut into quarters

2 ripe **avocados**, chopped

⅓ of a **cucumber**, peeled and chopped

½ an **orange pepper**, deseeded and chopped

2 tablespoons **dried cranberries**

1 tablespoon **toasted pecans**, roughly chopped

1. Rinse the quinoa under running cold water, and drain. Heat the oil in a pan and add the quinoa, stirring quickly for 1 minute. Add the water, then bring to the boil. Reduce the heat and simmer for about 20 minutes, until the quinoa is cooked but is still chewy. Remove from the heat.

2. While the quinoa is cooking, make the dressing by whisking all the ingredients together. Season well.

3. When the quinoa has cooled, put it into a serving bowl and stir in the dressing, followed by the rest of the ingredients. If you prefer, you can pack the mixture into a mould or ramekin and turn it out to serve.

**TIPS**

\* Other great additions:
- Cooked corn.
- Sliced cooked green beans.
- Cooked peas and broad beans.
- Feta cheese.
- Nuts and seeds.

# Puglian Bean Purée

## WITH PADRÓN PEPPERS

SERVES 4–6 • PREPARATION TIME: 15 MINUTES • COOKING TIME: 50 MINUTES • ♥ ✓ WF GF DF V

Traditionally this is known as *puré di fave* and is made with dried broad beans, which you can sometimes come across in Middle Eastern shops. This recipe uses dried cannellini beans (or haricots), which are easier to source. If you are lucky enough to find fava beans, reduce the bean cooking time.

200g **dried cannellini beans**, soaked overnight in lots of cold water

1 head of **garlic**

1 **red chilli**

**salt** and **freshly ground black pepper**

3–4 tablespoons **extra virgin olive oil**

1 tablespoon shredded **fresh sage leaves**

1 tablespoon **fennel seeds**, ground

½ teaspoon **dried chilli flakes**

2 cloves of **garlic**, crushed

200g **Padrón peppers**

### TIPS

* There are many variations of this purée but it is generally used as a vehicle for good olive oil. It is found on many menus in southern Italy, served with fried peppers (a small variety grown in the region) and braised wild chicory.

* To make this a 'fast' dish, use well-rinsed tinned beans.

* Try serving with braised chard or spinach.

* Makes great party food served on crostini with chopped fresh herbs.

1. Drain the soaked beans, then place them in a pan and cover with fresh cold water. Add the whole head of garlic, sliced in half across the centre, and the chilli. Bring to the boil, then reduce the heat and simmer for 30–40 minutes, until the beans are tender. Season and remove from the heat.

2. Drain the beans well and place them in a food processor. Squeeze out the soft garlic from each clove and add to the beans.

3. Heat 2 tablespoons of olive oil in a frying pan and add the sage, fennel seeds, chilli flakes and crushed garlic. Cook for 2 minutes over a medium heat, without letting the garlic brown, then add all the pan contents to the beans in the processor. Blitz until smooth. It may be necessary to add a little more olive oil in order to get a creamy consistency. Season.

4. Heat another tablespoon of oil in a frying pan over a medium heat and add the Padrón peppers. Sprinkle with salt, keep on stirring, and remove from the heat when the peppers are slightly browned. This should take 5 minutes.

5. Serve the bean purée with the Padrón peppers and some crusty bread.

# Using Fava Beans
## BY POLLY ROBINSON

Fava beans have been grown in Britain for thousands of years. When harvested and eaten young and fresh, they are better known as broad beans. Left to ripen and dry on the plant, fava beans were once an important part of the British diet, a vital source of protein until we started eating more meat and dairy products a few hundred years ago.

We still produce over half a million tonnes of fava beans every year, yet very few are eaten in this country: they are either fed to livestock or exported to the Middle East and North Africa. Meanwhile, Britain imports other beans – haricot, navy, kidney and others – that we've become more used to eating, but can't grow well in this country. It's time we started to put our own home-grown beans back on our plates!

> Polly was a vegetarian for 22 years so she knows a thing or two about beans. She now eats about 20 per cent meat. She is a great advocate for Suffolk produce and indulged her interest in good food by building Food Safari – a business that introduces people to new gastronomic experiences.
>
> JANE

POLLY, 1982

# Moroccan Bessara

SERVES 8 • PREPARATION TIME: 5 MINUTES • COOKING TIME: 50 MINUTES • ♥ WF GF DF V

This classic Moroccan dish, which can be served as either a dip or a soup, is based on a recipe from Moroccan chef Alia Al-Kasimi's website, www.cookingwithalia.com.

400g **split dried fava beans**, soaked in water overnight

3 large cloves of **garlic**

1.5 litres **water**

1 tablespoon **olive oil**

1 teaspoon **salt**

1 teaspoon **ground cumin**

1 teaspoon **paprika**

juice of 2 **lemons**

**TO SERVE**

**olive oil**

**ground cumin**

**paprika**

1. Place the drained fava beans and garlic in a large pan and just cover with the water. Put a lid on the pan and cook on a medium-high heat, skimming occasionally, for about 40 minutes, or until the beans are soft enough to purée easily.

2. Purée the beans and garlic, either by hand or in a food processor, according to your preferred texture. Stir in the oil, salt, spices and lemon juice. The consistency can be adjusted: for a thinner soup, mix in more hot water; for a thicker dip, boil the beans with less water.

3. Serve the bessara hot, drizzled with olive oil and sprinkled with cumin and paprika.

# Egyptian Falafels

MAKES ABOUT 16 (ENOUGH FOR 3–4) • PREPARATION TIME: 20 MINUTES, PLUS SOAKING & COOLING
COOKING TIME: 10 MINUTES • WF GF V

Surprisingly easy to cook from scratch, this traditional Arab food is delicious as a snack or meze. Authentic Egyptian falafels are made with fava beans, not chickpeas. Unlike many others, our recipe is both gluten-free and vegan – it contains no eggs, flour or breadcrumbs.

500g **split dried fava beans**, soaked in water overnight

a big bunch of **fresh coriander**

10 **fresh mint leaves**

1 **red chilli**

1 **red onion**

1 teaspoon **cayenne pepper**

1 teaspoon **ground cumin**

½ teaspoon **ground cinnamon**

3 pinches of **coarse salt**

3 pinches of **freshly ground black pepper**

grated zest of 2 **lemons**

**vegetable oil**, for deep-frying

**FOR THE MINT YOGHURT SAUCE**

8 **fresh mint leaves**

350g **natural yoghurt**

juice of ½ a **lemon**

1. You need to soak the beans overnight, but don't boil them, as all the cooking happens in the oil. Drain the beans after soaking.

2. Coarsely chop the herbs, chilli and onion. Put into a food processor with the beans, spices, salt, pepper and lemon zest, then pulse until fairly smooth – though not a paste.

3. Roll the mixture into ping-pong ball sized patties, place on a plate, then refrigerate for 30 minutes.

4. Meanwhile, prepare the yoghurt sauce. Finely chop the mint and mix in a bowl with the yoghurt and lemon juice. Season with salt and pepper, then refrigerate until ready to serve.

5. Heat enough vegetable oil in a wide deep pan big enough to fit all the patties in a single layer. When the oil is very hot (about 180°C), carefully lower the patties in the oil and deep-fry for 3–4 minutes, or until dark golden brown.

6. Drain briefly on kitchen paper and sprinkle lightly with salt. Serve the falafel with the yoghurt sauce, a lightly dressed salad and some pitta bread.

# Aubergine Jambalaya

SERVES 4 • PREPARATION TIME: 10 MINUTES • COOKING TIME: 30 MINUTES • ♥ ✓ WF GF DF V

This signature dish from Louisiana varies throughout the state. You can buy a Creole seasoning mix, but it is more fun to mix your own. Brown rice takes longer to cook, which can be used if time is on your side.

1 tablespoon **olive oil**

1 **onion**, chopped

1 **red pepper**, finely chopped

2 sticks of **celery**, finely chopped

2 cloves of **garlic**, crushed

**herbs**: 1 **bay leaf**, a pinch of **dried oregano**, a pinch of **dried thyme**

a pinch of **dried chilli flakes**

1 teaspoon **sweet smoked paprika**

220g **long-grain rice**

1 **aubergine**, cut into 1cm dice

1 tablespoon **tomato purée**

1 x 400g tin of **chopped tomatoes**

**salt** and **freshly ground black pepper**

400ml **vegetable stock**

1. Heat the oil in a large pan, then add the onion, pepper and celery and cook for 5 minutes over a medium heat.

2. Add the garlic, herbs and spices and cook for 2 minutes.

3. Add the rice, aubergine, tomato purée and tinned tomatoes. Stir well, season and cook for a further 2 minutes.

4. Add the stock, bring to a simmer, then cover the pan and cook for 20 minutes. Turn off the heat and leave to steam for 5 minutes. Fluff up the rice and serve with a freshly dressed green salad.

**VARIATIONS**

✿ Other vegetables can be added to this halfway through the cooking time, such as sweetcorn, peas, and French or broad beans.

✿ Smoked tofu or tempeh could be used instead of aubergine pieces.

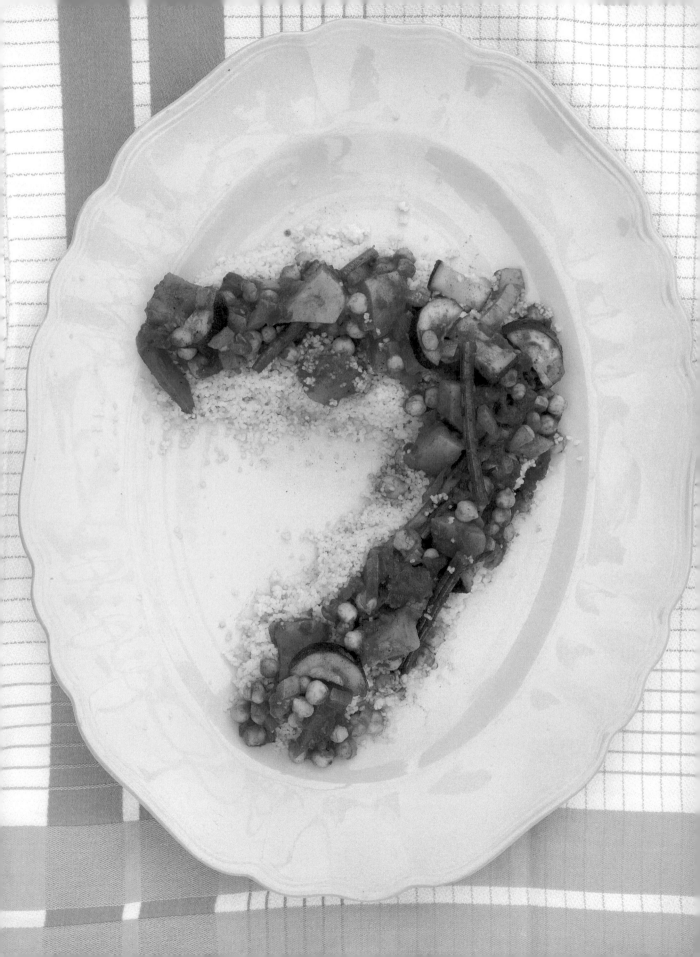

# Couscous with Seven Vegetables

SERVES 4 • PREPARATION TIME: 15 MINUTES • COOKING TIME: 40 MINUTES • ♥ DF V

In Morocco, couscous is traditionally often served with seven types of vegetables. Any variation on the seven will suffice, but it is important to add the vegetables in stages, as they will take different times to cook – that way the result won't be mush.

1 tablespoon **olive oil**

1 **onion**, diced

1 teaspoon **ground ginger**

1 teaspoon **ground cinnamon**

2 teaspoons **rose harissa**

1 x 400g tin of **chopped tomatoes**

1kg **mixed vegetables** (six types – we used **squash**, **turnips**, **parsnips**, **carrots**, all peeled and cut into small chunks; **courgettes**, halved and sliced; **French beans**, trimmed)

100ml **water**

**salt** and **freshly ground black pepper**

1 x 400g tin of **chickpeas**, drained

juice of 1 **orange**

chopped **fresh coriander and mint**

**FOR THE COUSCOUS**

200g **couscous**

1 tablespoon **olive oil**

400ml **boiling water**

1. Heat the oil in a large pan, then add the onion and cook over a medium heat for 5 minutes.

2. Add the spices and harissa and stir well. Cook for 1 minute, then add the tomatoes with their juice. Bring up to a simmer and tip in the squash and the root vegetables. Add the 100ml water, stir and season well. Bring up to a simmer, then cover and cook over a low heat for 15 minutes, or until the vegetables are almost tender.

3. Add the rest of the vegetables and cook for a further 10 minutes, pouring in a little more water if the mixture starts to stick.

4. When all the vegetables are tender, add the drained chickpeas, the orange juice, then season and mix well.

5. To cook the couscous, put the grain into a bowl and rub in the olive oil and a little salt. Pour over the boiling water, then cover tightly with clingfilm and leave to steam for 10 minutes.

6. Fluff up the couscous with a fork, sprinkle with the chopped herbs, then serve with the vegetables.

**TIPS**

* Traditionally dried fruit and nuts are added to meat tagines, so try adding sliced dried apricots or dates for an authentic flavour. Toasted almonds, pine nuts or cashews are also nice additions.

* The types of vegetables used can be varied, but it is good to try and maintain a balance of root and green veg. Other vegetables you could use include: cauliflower, broccoli, spinach, kale, celeriac or mushrooms.

# TIPS FOR COOKING WITH PULSES

## SOAKING DRIED BEANS
### (THIS DOES NOT APPLY TO RED KIDNEY BEANS)

Usually, dried beans are soaked overnight, but if you forget you can still go ahead using the following method (lentils and split peas do not need to be soaked overnight):

1. Put the beans into a pan and cover with lots of cold water. Bring to the boil, then leave to sit for an hour.

2. Drain, then cover with cold water and start the recipe as if the beans had been soaked.

## TO COOK SOAKED BEANS

1. Place the drained beans in a pan and cover with water.

2. Slice a whole bulb of garlic in half lengthways and add both halves to the pan along with a sprig of rosemary or sage (depending what you are using the beans for). Bring to the boil, then reduce the heat and simmer for anything from 40 minutes to an hour, until the beans are just cooked. During the cooking process, make sure that the beans are always covered with water.

3. Season the cooked beans very well and add some olive oil. Remove the bulbs of garlic and squeeze the soft garlic pulp into the bean mix and stir to combine. Discard the skins. Allow to cool, and keep in a sealed container in the fridge. The beans will be very tasty, well-seasoned and garlicky and ready to be used in soups, stews, dips, fritters or snacks. They will keep very well in the fridge in their cooking liquor for up to 3 days.

(Some dried beans can be very old and seem to take an awful long time to cook … a pinch of bicarbonate of soda during the cooking process can help to soften them, but only do this as a last resort, because they can become mushy.)

### SOME SIMPLE DISHES USING PULSES

* **With braised greens:** Braise blanched kale with garlic and chilli. Add drained cannellini beans and cook together for a few minutes. This mixture can be served as it is, as a side, or blended together with good olive oil and served on crostini as a snack. The same can be done with lentils and chard/spinach and chickpeas (see recipe opposite).

* **In salads:** Add haricot beans to a mixture of roast cauliflower and grilled leeks, dress with balsamic vinegar, olive oil and a grating of vegetarian Parmesan-style cheese.

* Puy lentils make a great addition to salads, especially roasted beetroot, feta and mint.

* Add borlotti beans to cooked farro and vegetables to make a delicious salad.

* Bitter leaves like escarole and radicchio can be braised and added to beans for a soup or tossed in dressing and added to lentils for a warm salad.

* **As a snack:** Chickpeas make a great snack to serve with drinks. Drain cooked chickpeas and dry well. Toss in a little olive oil, then roast in the oven at 220°C/425°F/gas mark 7 for 30 minutes, shaking the tray every 10 minutes. Remove from the oven and toss in a mixture of cayenne pepper, smoked paprika and salt.

# Braised Chard

## WITH CHICKPEAS & CARROTS

SERVES 4 • PREPARATION TIME: 15 MINUTES • COOKING TIME: 25 MINUTES • ♥ ✓ WF GF DF V

There are many versions of this dish. It can be served hot or at room temperature.

2 tablespoons **olive oil**

1 **onion**, finely chopped

200g **carrots**,
cut into rough 1cm dice

1 **celery heart**,
cut into rough 1cm dice

3 cloves of **garlic**, crushed

1 **dried chilli**, crumbled

100ml **white wine**

200g tinned **chopped tomatoes**

**salt** and **freshly ground
black pepper**

300g **chard**

1 x 400g tin of **chickpeas**,
rinsed and drained

1 tablespoon **chopped parsley**

**extra virgin olive oil**

1. Heat the oil in a large pan and cook the onion over a medium heat for 5 minutes. Add the carrots and celery, mix well and cook for a further 10 minutes.

2. Add the garlic and chilli and turn up the heat. Stir for 1 minute, then tip in the wine and tomatoes. Cook over a medium heat for a further 5 minutes, until the sauce is just coating the vegetables. Season well.

3. Wash the chard well and separate the leaves from the stalks. Chop the stalks finely. Bring a pan of salted water to the boil and cook the stalks for 2 minutes, then tip in the leaves and cook for a further minute. Drain the chard and refresh under cold running water. Squeeze out excess moisture and chop roughly.

4. Stir the chard and chickpeas into the vegetable mix and warm through gently. Season well. Sprinkle with parsley, drizzle with good olive oil and serve.

**VARIATIONS**

✿ Spinach or kale can be substituted for the chard.

✿ Other pulses can be used instead of chickpeas. Try Puy lentils, borlotti beans or cannellini beans.

# CHILDREN

LEON

# Pat's Broad Bean Burgers

MAKES 6 • PREPARATION TIME: 10 MINUTES • COOKING TIME: 25 MINUTES • ♥ ✓ WF GF DF V

These were developed by my friend Katie's mum, Pat, to encourage her children to eat broad beans. It is very important to allow the mixture to stand for at least 10 minutes once the oats have been added, so that it all binds together.

1 tablespoon **olive oil**

1 **onion**, finely chopped

2 cloves of **garlic**, crushed

leaves from approximately 4 sprigs of **fresh thyme**

600g **broad beans**, podded weight (fine to use frozen)

50g **porridge oats**

1 large **egg**, beaten

1 tablespoon chopped **fresh flat-leaf parsley**

2 teaspoons **Marmite**

**salt** and **freshly ground black pepper**

**olive oil**, for frying

1. Heat the oil in a frying pan and add the onion, garlic and thyme leaves. Cook over a low heat for 10 minutes.

2. Bring a pan of salted water to the boil, then add the broad beans and blanch for 3 minutes, or until tender. Drain well.

3. Mash the broad beans by hand or in a food processor, then transfer to a bowl and add the onion mixture and the rest of the ingredients, apart from the frying oil. Mix well, then allow to sit for at least 10 minutes, so that the oats can soak up the egg. Season well.

4. Shape the mixture into 6 burger shapes and shallow-fry gently in oil until browned on each side. Drain on kitchen paper and serve.

**TIPS**

* For an adult version of these, omit the Marmite and add chopped mint and lemon zest.

* These burgers may seem very wet when you shape them, but they will hold their shape when fried. If you still have problems, add a little gram or rice flour to the mixture.

PAT GETTING READY FOR A DANCE CLASS, SOUTH SHIELDS, 1952

# Simon's Potato Wedges

SERVES 4–6 • PREPARATION TIME: 10 MINUTES • COOKING TIME: 45 MINUTES • ♥ WF DF V

Love it or hate it, Marmite used in this way really gives great roast wedges. It's up to you how much you use and how often you add it during the cooking of the tatties.

3 tablespoons **olive oil**

1.25kg **floury potatoes**

**salt** and **freshly ground black pepper**

1 tablespoon **semolina flour**

a good squeeze of squeezy **Marmite**

1. Heat the oven to 200°C/400°F/gas mark 6. Put the oil into a roasting tray and place in the oven to heat up.

2. Peel the potatoes and cut in half, then cut each half into thick wedges. Place in a pan and cover with cold water. Bring to the boil, then remove from the heat, drain and shake in a colander. Season, then sprinkle with the semolina flour and shake again until well coated.

3. Tip the potato wedges into the hot oil in the roasting tray and turn them around so that they are well coated. Squeeze over about a tablespoon of Marmite and shake the tray.

4. Return the tray to the oven and cook for 20 minutes. Check the potatoes and turn them over, giving them a stir before returning them to the oven. At this point more Marmite can be added, to taste. Roast for a further 20 minutes, or until the wedges are browned and crisp, then serve.

SIMON WITH LYNDY REDDING, SOUTH BAY BEACH, SCARBOROUGH, 1971

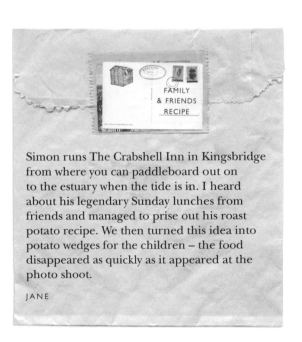

FAMILY & FRIENDS RECIPE

Simon runs The Crabshell Inn in Kingsbridge from where you can paddleboard out on to the estuary when the tide is in. I heard about his legendary Sunday lunches from friends and managed to prise out his roast potato recipe. We then turned this idea into potato wedges for the children – the food disappeared as quickly as it appeared at the photo shoot.

JANE

# Mima's Martian Meteors

MAKES ABOUT 30 SMALL METEORS • PREPARATION TIME: 10 MINUTES
COOKING TIME: 10 MINUTES • ♥ ✓ WF GF DF V

Any root vegetable can be used in these, along with grated courgettes and other veg.

500g **mixed root vegetables**
(we used a mixture of **swede**,
**parsnip**, **celeriac** and **carrot**)

100g **gram flour**

1 teaspoon **baking powder**

1 teaspoon **garam masala**

approximately 200ml **soda water**

**salt** and **freshly ground
black pepper**

**sunflower oil**, for frying

1. Peel the vegetables and grate them, either using a grater or the attachment in a food processor.

2. Sift the gram flour into a large bowl with the baking powder and garam masala.

3. Slowly pour in the soda water, whisking to make a smooth batter with the consistency of double cream. Season well.

4. Add the grated vegetables to the batter and mix thoroughly with your hands.

5. Heat the oil to 180°C in a deep-fryer or large pan. Carefully drop in walnut-sized balls of the mixture and deep-fry for a few minutes until golden brown. Lift out with a slotted spoon and drain on kitchen paper. Serve.

## TIPS

* These fritters are good served with either Mint Yoghurt Sauce (see page 129) or Tahini Dressing (see page 81) – or just with ketchup.

* Try adding fresh herbs to the mixture, such as parsley, chives and chervil.

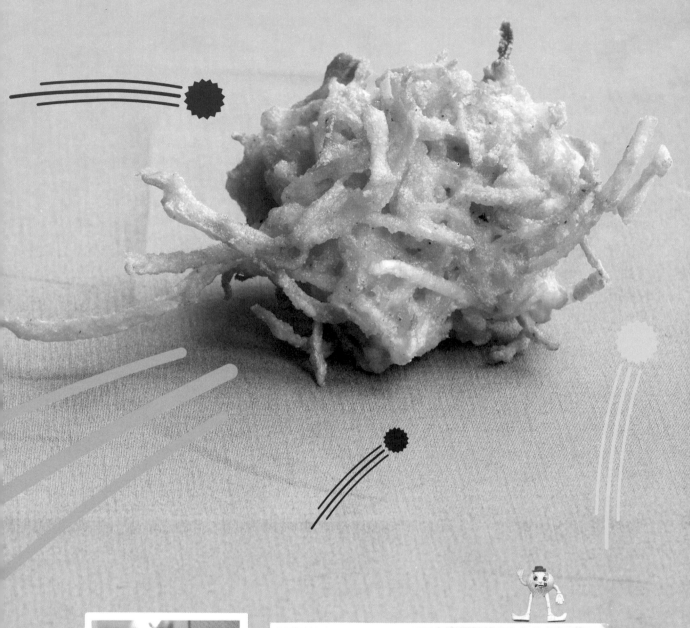

MIMA, HATTIE & THEIR FATHER, JEREMY,
LONDON 1976

There are many ways to get children to eat their
vegetables. There is the school of thought that
recommends making vegetables taste good and letting
them compete fair and square with chips and pudding.
I like this theory, but in practice have fallen back on
subterfuge and brainwashing. Millions of years of
evolution have given our children an irresistible yearning
for sweet, energy-rich foods – we need all the tools at our
disposal to fight back. My wife Mima invented this recipe.
Not only does it hide the vegetables beneath a crispy
exterior, but it has a killer name to encourage a first bite.
They also taste really good.

HENRY

# Fresh Orecchiette

## WITH TOMATO SAUCE

SERVES 4 • PREPARATION TIME: 20 MINUTES • COOKING TIME: 8 MINUTES • DF V

The addition of the semolina flour makes these 'little ears' easy to form. They can be loads of fun to make with your children. The pasta shapes can be used fresh or frozen in bags. We have provided a recipe for a very simple tomato sauce, but you can also serve these with Pea & Spinach (see page 108), Creamed Kale (see page 234) or purple sprouting broccoli braised in olive oil with chilli and garlic.

300g **semolina flour**, plus a little for dusting

300g **'00' pasta flour**

**salt**

approximately 500ml **tepid water**

1. Sift the flours and salt into a large bowl and make a well in the middle. Add the water slowly, a little at a time, until a soft dough is formed.

2. Place the dough on a floured work surface and knead it for 10 minutes, until smooth. Cover and set aside for 15 minutes.

3. Roll the dough into long strips about 2cm thick. Cut across the strips into 1cm pieces and press the centre of each piece with your thumb to form a saucer shape.

4. Place each piece on a tray dusted with semolina flour and set aside until ready to use.

5. Bring a large pan of salted water to the boil, add the orecchiette and cook for about 7–8 minutes, or until al dente. Toss with your chosen sauce.

When we asked the children from my son's local school to make this pasta, I had to stop myself insisting on shapes of the perfect thickness. Even though they were all shaped like wonky ears, once they were cooked and tossed in tomato sauce they were wolfed down in seconds. A lesson to us all when cooking: do not let a desire for perfection get in the way of making something good.
JANE

# Tomato Sauce

2 tablespoons **olive oil**

10 cloves of **garlic**, thinly sliced

1 **dried chilli** (optional)

2 x 440g tins of **chopped tomatoes**

a pinch of **sugar**

**salt** and **freshly ground black pepper**

1. Heat the oil in a large saucepan and add the finely sliced garlic and the chilli, if using. Stir over a medium heat for about 1 minute without browning.

2. Tip in the tinned tomatoes, add the sugar, then stir and turn up the heat and bring to a simmer. Cook over a medium heat for about 20 minutes, making sure the sauce does not catch on the base of the pan. The sauce can be simmered over a lower heat for longer, if you are doing this ahead of time.

3. Season well, then use an immersion blender briefly to make a quick tomato sauce.

**VARIATIONS**

❀ Fresh basil can be added at the beginning and end of cooking.

❀ Dried porcini mushrooms and rosemary can be added with the garlic.

❀ Chopped rosemary and fresh chilli make a great addition.

❀ Add a splash of balsamic vinegar, a knob of butter, basil and pecorino.

❀ Add a dash of cream at the end of cooking, and some vegetarian Parmesan-style cheese.

# Jossy's Beetroot Hummus

SERVES 4–6 • PREPARATION TIME: 10 MINUTES • COOKING TIME: 30–60 MINUTES • ♥ ✓ WF GF DF V

Very easy, very good – wonderfully scarlet. Great for children when they realize the colour their teeth and lips (and everything else) will become when they eat it.

500g **raw beetroot**

1–2 large cloves of **garlic**

**sea salt** and **freshly ground black pepper**

1 x 400g tin of **chickpeas**, drained

juice of ½ a **large lemon**

2–3 tablespoons **extra virgin olive oil**

a large handful of **fresh flat leaf parsley**, chopped

## TIPS

\* An alternative way of preparing and cooking the beetroot for this recipe, is to peel the beetroot and cut it into chunks, toss in olive oil, then season with salt and pepper. Place in a roasting tin, cover with foil and roast in a medium oven (160°C/325°F/gas mark 3) for 40 minutes, or until tender.

1. Bring a large pan of unsalted water to the boil. Wash the beetroot thoroughly, then add it to the pan and boil until it feels soft when you insert a sharp knife – 30 minutes to 1 hour, depending on the size of the beetroot. Meanwhile, peel the garlic, chop roughly and purée using a pestle and mortar with a little sea salt.

2. When the beetroot is tender, drain and place under cold running water until you can peel off the skin and take away the stem part without burning your fingers. Chop the beetroot roughly and put them into a food processor with the puréed garlic, drained chickpeas and lemon juice. Whizz until smooth. Leave the mixture in the processor until almost cold. Then, with the machine running, add the olive oil gradually.

3. Finally, season to taste with sea salt and freshly ground black pepper and stir in most of the chopped parsley, reserving a little for a garnish. Turn into a serving bowl and sprinkle with the reserved parsley.

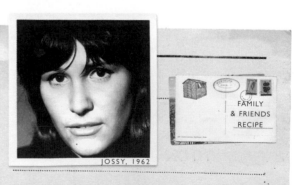

JOSSY, 1962

FAMILY & FRIENDS RECIPE

When I was young, I had a friend called Bruno who claimed to have 'food phobias'. This drove my mum mad. She would always try to catch him out. She would say things like: 'So you have a food phobia to eggs? Then you can't have ice cream. Who else would like some?' Bruno was six years old. My mum made my friends try all foods once, even when they professed to hate them. On account of inventive dishes like this hummus, she won these battles more often than she lost them. 'I told you he would like *my* carrots!'

HENRY

# Li'l Bob's Black Bean Chocolate Chilli

This chilli can be served either in a wrap, with grated cheese and chopped tomato salsa, or with rice. Kidney beans or any white beans can be substituted for the black beans.

1 tablespoon **olive oil**

1 **onion**, finely chopped

1 **red pepper**, finely chopped

1 **aubergine**, cut into small dice

½ teaspoon **ground cumin**

½ teaspoon **ground coriander**

1 mild **red chilli**, chopped

1 clove of **garlic**, crushed

200g **chopped tomatoes** (tinned are fine)

2 tablespoons **soy sauce**

1 x 300g tin of **black beans**

**salt** and **freshly ground black pepper**

25g **dark chocolate** (or **chilli chocolate**), broken up

1. Heat the oil in a large shallow frying pan, add the onion and red pepper and cook for 5 minutes over a medium heat.

2. Add the diced aubergine and continue frying for a further 5 minutes, stirring to prevent the mixture from sticking.

3. Sprinkle over the spices, chilli and garlic, turn up the heat and stir for a minute, then tip in the tomatoes and soy sauce. Simmer for 10 minutes, or until the aubergine is tender.

4. Add the beans to the pan and cook for a few more minutes, then season well and remove from the heat. Add the chocolate pieces, stir until they have just melted, then serve.

Bob Granleese is a food journalist, brilliant cook and an old friend of Jane. Henry met him recently on a fishing trip over the Skerries sand bank in Start Bay in Devon. They didn't catch anything, but discovered a mutual appreciation of Shipwreck – a local cider brandy.

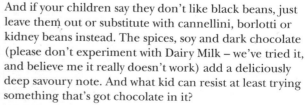

Aubergines aren't exactly British children's favourite veg (well they're not my children's anyway), they say they look like giant purple slugs and that they taste pretty much how they imagine a giant purple slug would taste, too; slimy and horrible. This is the only way I can get them to eat this staple of the southern Mediterranean. The idea is that, by dicing the raw aubergine so it looks like large bits of mince, then frying it in a little olive oil first, it holds its shape, rather than disintegrating into mush, and adds texture, bite and body to the finished dish.

And if your children say they don't like black beans, just leave them out or substitute with cannellini, borlotti or kidney beans instead. The spices, soy and dark chocolate (please don't experiment with Dairy Milk – we've tried it, and believe me it really doesn't work) add a deliciously deep savoury note. And what kid can resist at least trying something that's got chocolate in it?

BOB

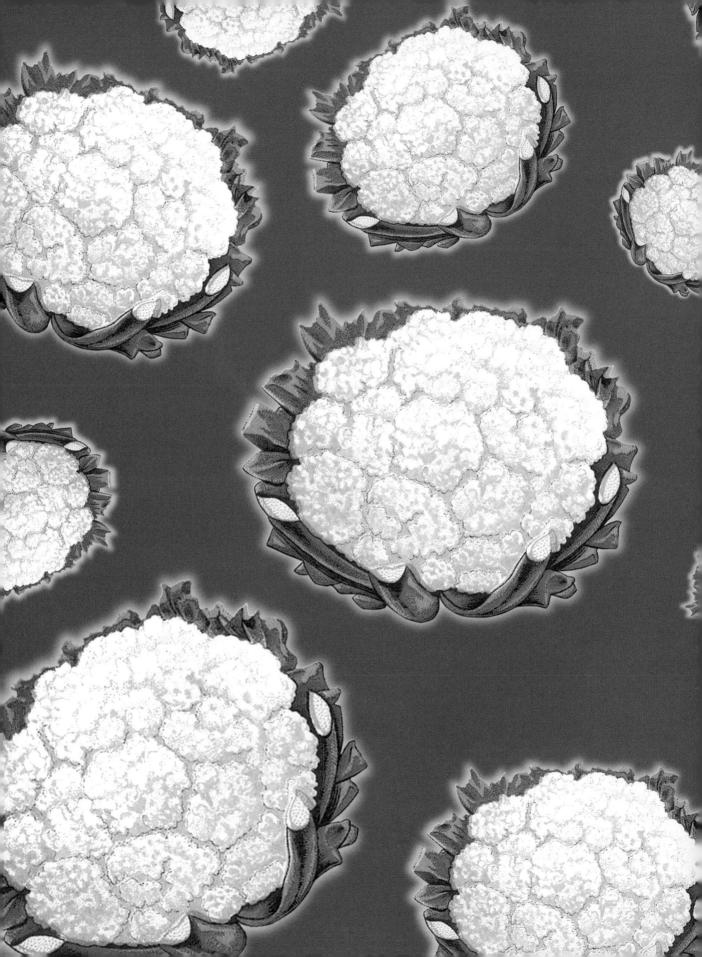

# PIES & BAKES

LEON

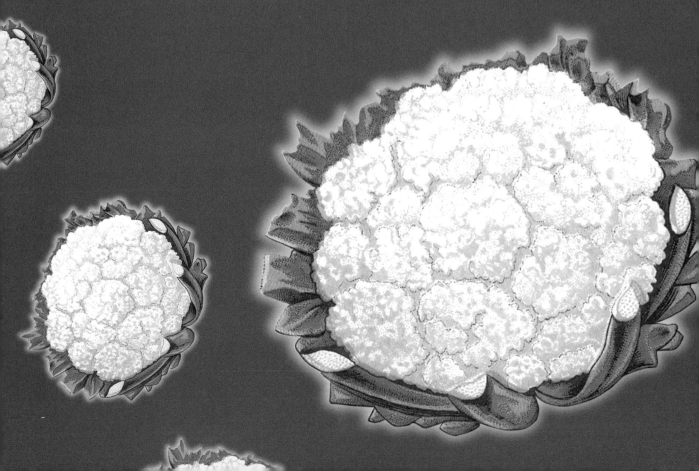

# Baked Spinach, Squash & Blue Cheese

SERVES 4–6 • PREPARATION TIME: 15 MINUTES • COOKING TIME: 40–60 MINUTES • ✓ WF GF V ⓥ

A simple autumnal bake combining some of our favourite flavours.

400g **squash**, peeled and cut into 1–2cm dice

1 tablespoon **olive oil**

6 **fresh sage leaves**, shredded

300g **spinach**

1 **egg**

100ml **double cream**

75g **blue cheese** (such as Gorgonzola), crumbled

**salt** and **freshly ground black pepper**

40g **toasted walnuts**, chopped

1. Heat the oven to 200°C/400°F/gas mark 6. Put the squash into a roasting tray and toss with the oil and sage. Roast in the oven for 20–30 minutes, until tender.

2. Meanwhile, bring a large pan of salted water to the boil. Add the spinach and blanch for 30 seconds, then drain and refresh under cold water. Drain again and squeeze out any excess moisture. Chop roughly.

3. Beat the egg with the cream in a mixing bowl and add the spinach and the crumbled cheese. Season well.

4. When the squash is cooked, add it to the spinach mixture and transfer it all to a baking dish.

5. Lower the oven temperature to 140°C/275°F/ gas mark 1 and bake for around 20–30 minutes, or until almost firm to the touch but still with a slight wobble.

6. When ready, sprinkle with the walnuts and serve.

**TIPS**

* This makes a great filling for a pasty, or is equally good cooked on a puff pastry base, or baked on bruschetta.

* Spiced pecans are a lovely alternative to walnuts – toss the nuts in a little oil and sprinkle with salt and cayenne pepper, then cook in a preheated oven, 180°C/350°F/gas mark 4 for 5 minutes. This same method can be used to liven up any tired nut.

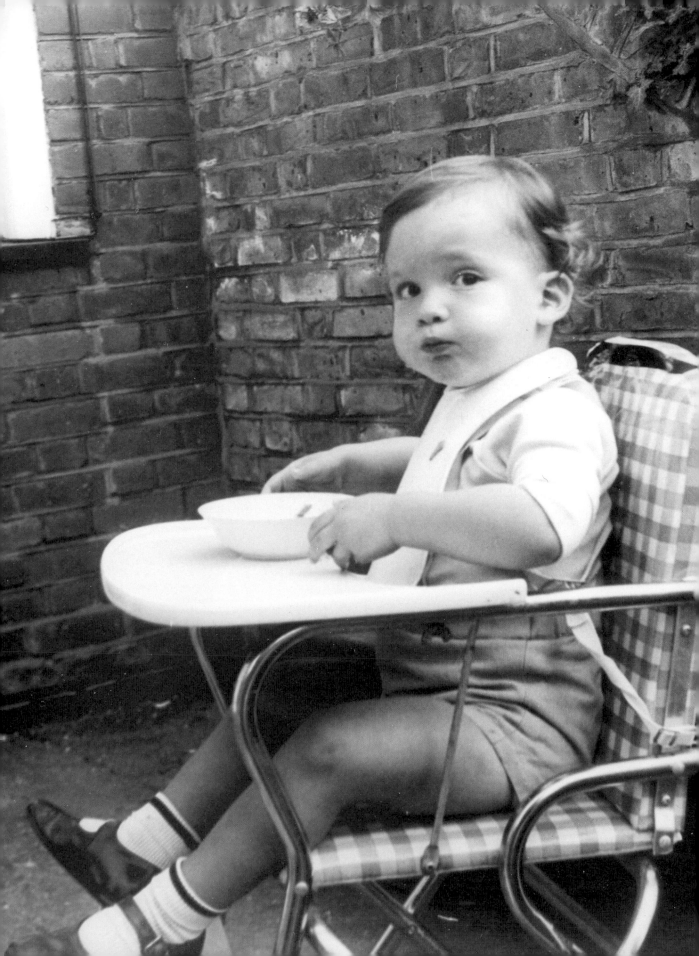

# Giles's Egg & Potato Pie

For two people as a main dish. Needs no accompaniment. Green salad if you must. Can be used as a side but I think that's a shame. It is a simple earthy glory in its own right. I think it is a Slovak dish. Because my Grandma, herself a Slovak dish in her time, taught it to me.

Take six eggs. Boil them to hard but not so hard that they become difficult to peel.

Boil as many floury potatoes as you need to make three layers in a medium-ish sort of dish. Maybe 500g? Who knows. Err on the side of too many and if you have some left over throw them at the neighbourhood cats. Only parboil them. They must hold together for slicing. Then slice them as thinly as you can. That may not be very thin. It doesn't matter.

Slice your eggs with an egg slicer. You don't have an egg slicer? Then go and buy one! The whole point of this dish is to create a use for your stupid pointless egg slicer. It's such fun slicing eggs with one!

Have plenty of butter, about half a pack. Make lots of gobbets and chuck them in the bottom of an ovenproof dish. If it's warm they'll melt a bit and coat it nicely.

Oh, turn the oven up high. Say, 200°C/400°F/gas mark 6.

Layer of spuds in the pot. More gobs of butter. LOTS of butter! Salt and freshly ground black pepper. Lots of it.

Layer of eggs. Using three eggs' worth.

Layer of spuds. More butter. LOTS. Also salt and pepper.

Layer of eggs.

Last layer of spuds. LOTS OF BUTTER. Salt and pepper.

Into the very hot oven. Half an hour. To really bake everything together. The bottom layer of spuds should be practically deep-frying down there. And the top layer browning nicely. When it's done, an eating knife will go in and out easily without sticking.

Leave it 5 minutes to relax.

Spoon it out and eat that mofo! Add nothing. Never try to improve it. No garlic, no onion, no sausage, no nothing.

And no ketchup!

You have to taste that spud and eggy heaven (it goes without saying that the better your pots, eggs, butter, salt and pepper, the better your pie will be).

Ketchup is allowed with seconds however. As it can all get a bit much otherwise.

My friend Giles Coren is a really excellent cook and generous host. This carefree exterior, however, belies a very precise nature, particularly when it comes to cooking – so change the recipe at your peril.

HENRY

# Courgette & Tomato Gratin

SERVES 4 • PREPARATION TIME: 15 MINUTES • COOKING TIME: 35 MINUTES • ♥ WF GF V

A classic gratin using summer vegetables.

400g **ripe beef tomatoes**

400g **courgettes**

5 tablespoons **olive oil**

1 clove of **garlic**, crushed

2 tablespoons **vegetarian Parmesan-style cheese**

1 tablespoon **polenta**

2 tablespoons chopped **mixed fresh herbs** (basil, chives, oregano, parsley)

**salt** and **freshly ground black pepper**

1. Heat the oven to 180°C/350°F/gas mark 4. Core the tomatoes and slice them thinly.

2. Top and tail the courgettes and slice them thinly lengthways. Put them into a bowl and toss with a 3 tablespoons of the olive oil. Heat a grill or griddle pan until hot, and grill the courgette slices on both sides until tender.

3. Put the garlic, Parmesan, polenta and herbs into a bowl and mix together.

4. Oil an ovenproof dish and start layering the veg, starting with a layer of courgettes, then a layer of tomatoes and a sprinkling of the cheesy herb mix. Season each layer and drizzle with the remaining olive oil.

5. Finish with a layer of the cheesy herb mix and bake in the oven for about 30 minutes, until golden on top.

**TIPS**

* Try frying aubergine slices and use instead of the courgettes.

* For cheese lovers, extra cheese can be added with the Parmesan ... we like to use a little grated fontina or mozzarella.

# Root Vegetable Stew with Baked Dumplings

SERVES 4 • PREPARATION TIME: 25 MINUTES • COOKING TIME: 45 MINUTES • DF V

This is a wintry stew in which a variety of seasonal roots can be used, although we always include swede because it seems to create the best gravy. The baked dumplings are an optional addition.

40g **dried porcini mushrooms**

500ml **boiling water**

1 tablespoon **olive oil**

1 **onion**, finely chopped

1 clove of **garlic**, crushed

800–900g **mixed root vegetables** (**swede**, **turnips**, **carrots**, **celeriac**), peeled and cut into 2cm square chunks

a sprig of **fresh thyme**

1 **bay leaf**

200ml **red wine**

2 teaspoons **sugar**

### FOR THE DUMPLINGS

75g good-quality **vegetarian suet**

150g **self-raising flour**, sifted

**salt** and **freshly ground black pepper**

1 **egg**

2 tablespoons **creamed horseradish**

### TIPS

* Serve with creamy mash and braised kale.

* For the perfect accompaniment to a poached egg, make the sauce with only a quarter of the veg (diced very small) but use the same amounts of red wine and porcini.

* Try using ale or Guinness instead of red wine.

1. Put the porcini into a bowl, pour over the boiling water and leave to soak for 30 minutes. Drain, reserving the soaking liquid, squeeze out excess water and chop the mushrooms finely.

2. Heat the oil in a large pan. Add the onion and garlic and cook for 1 minute, then add the porcini and stir well. Tip in the mixed root vegetable chunks, then turn up the heat and cook for 2 minutes, stirring to prevent the vegetables from sticking.

3. Add the porcini soaking liquid to the pan, along with the herbs, and cook over a medium heat to reduce the volume of liquid by half.

4. Add the red wine and sugar, turn up the heat again to a rapid boil and cook for 20–25 minutes, stirring occasionally and reducing the sauce to thicken it while the vegetables are cooking. If the sauce gets too thick, add a little water.

5. Meanwhile, heat the oven to 190°C/375°F/ gas mark 5. Put the suet and flour into a bowl and mix together. Season well.

6. Whisk the egg in a bowl with 1 tablespoon of cold water and add to the suet mix, using your hands to bring it together to form a soft dough and adding more water if required. The dough needs to be fairly wet for the best results.

7. Divide the dough into 8 small balls. Using your finger, stuff a little of the horseradish into the centre of each ball and re-seal the dough.

8. Pour the root vegetable stew into a casserole dish. Dot the dumplings over the top and place in the oven for 15 minutes, or until they are browned on top.

JANE'S LITTLE DUMPLING DAVID, 2003, SAMOA

# Jerusalem Artichokes, Mushrooms & Radicchio 'In a Bag'

SERVES 4 • PREPARATION TIME: 15 MINUTES • COOKING TIME: 20 MINUTES • ✓ WF GF V

Cooking *en papillote* is a method usually used for fish or seafood. But, it also works really well with scented Jerusalem artichokes – the flavours are sealed in and mingle together in a way that no other cooking method could achieve.

1 small head of **radicchio**

500g **Jerusalem artichokes**, peeled

250g **chestnut mushrooms**, quartered

2 cloves of **garlic**, crushed

2 teaspoons **fresh thyme leaves**

1 tablespoon **olive oil**

**salt** and **freshly ground black pepper**

30g **butter**, cut into small pieces

approximately 50ml **white wine**

2 tablespoons **balsamic vinegar**

80g **goat's cheese**, crumbled

1 tablespoon chopped **fresh parsley**

**TIPS**

* You can experiment with this method using any vegetables. For example, new potatoes are lovely tossed with oil, garlic and herbs and cooked in a bag for about 40 minutes. It is surprising how fast the whole process is compared with roasting.

1. Heat the oven to 200°C/400°F/gas mark 6.

2. Place a large baking tray in the oven to heat up (you may need two smaller trays, on separate shelves, if your oven is small).

3. Peel off the outer withered leaves from the radicchio and discard. Cut the radicchio into quarters and cut each quarter into thin wedges. Slice the peeled Jerusalem artichokes about 5mm thick.

4. Put the radicchio wedges into a large bowl with the artichokes, mushrooms, garlic, thyme and olive oil and mix together. Season well. Dot with the butter, then pour over the wine and balsamic vinegar and mix again.

5. Tear off 4 oblong pieces of kitchen foil or baking parchment (about 30 x 20cm) and place them on a clean work surface. Divide the vegetable mixture between the foil, placing it in the centre. Fold over the foil and seal the edges by crimping them as though you were making 4 big pasties. Spoon any liquid left in the vegetable bowl over the vegetables before completely sealing the bags. It is important that there are no holes in your bags, as the vegetables need to steam inside.

6. Carefully slide the parcels on to the hot baking tray(s). Bake in the oven for about 20 minutes. The parcels should puff up and the artichokes should be tender inside.

7. To serve, open the parcels, crumble over the goat's cheese and sprinkle with parsley.

# Cauliflower Cheese

SERVES 4–6 • PREPARATION TIME: 10 MINUTES • COOKING TIME: 30 MINUTES • ✓ WF GF V

The recipe below is a very quick version that requires no béchamel sauce but is just as delicious (and is wheat free).

1 head of **cauliflower**

1 tablespoon **olive oil**

2 teaspoons **maple syrup**

**salt** and **freshly ground black pepper**

350g **crème fraîche**

50g **Gruyère cheese**, grated

2 teaspoons **Dijon mustard**

1 tablespoon grated **vegetarian Parmesan-style cheese**

1 tablespoon **chopped fresh chives**

1. Heat the oven to 170°C/325°F/gas mark 3. Cut the caulifower into florets and toss them in a bowl with the oil and maple syrup. Season well. Transfer to a gratin dish or roasting tray and cook in the oven for 15–20 minutes, or until the cauliflower is just tender.

2. Put the crème fraîche, Gruyère and mustard into a bowl and stir to combine. Tip in the roasted cauli, mix until well coated and season.

3. Sprinkle with the Parmesan and put back into the oven for another 10 minutes, until golden. Sprinkle with the chives and serve.

**VARIATIONS**

✿ Substitute blue cheese for the Gruyère and add chopped toasted walnuts to the sauce for a different result.

✿ To make a richer dish, whisk an egg yolk into the crème fraîche, then after cooking drizzle with truffle oil.

✿ For an alternative topping, mix the Parmesan with chopped fresh herbs, breadcrumbs, crushed garlic and lemon zest, then sprinkle over before the final 10 minutes cooking time.

✿ Add some blanched leeks to the cauliflower before the final roasting.

✿ Add cooked chopped spinach and lots of fresh herbs, such as tarragon and parsley, to the cauli before roasting.

# Roast Head of Cauliflower

SERVES 6 • PREPARATION TIME: 10 MINUTES • COOKING TIME: 35 MINUTES • ✓ WF GF V

Roasting the cauliflower whole intensifies the flavour and makes quite an impact when serving. It is a mile away from the overcooked boiled cauli that many of us have experienced in the past!

1 head of **cauliflower**

40g **butter**, softened

½ teaspoon **smoked paprika**

grated **nutmeg**

1 clove of **garlic**, crushed

**salt** and **freshly ground black pepper**

**FOR THE DRESSING**

2 tablespoons **golden raisins**

2 tablespoons **capers**

1 tablespoon **olive oil**

1 tablespoon **sherry vinegar**

1 tablespoon chopped **fresh flat-leaf parsley**

**TIPS**

* To speed up the cooking, the cauliflower can be cut up into quarters and roasted but you will loose the impressive presentation of serving the cauliflower whole.

* An alternative topping is a salsa made from chopped boiled egg, tarragon, parsley and almonds, dressed with garlic, vinegar and olive oil; or try the dressing from Leeks Vinaigrette (see page 202).

1. Heat the oven to 220°C/425°F/gas mark 7. Take a large sheet of kitchen foil, big enough to wrap round the cauliflower, and place it on a baking tray. Trim the base of the cauliflower and place it on the foil.

2. Put the softened butter into a bowl and mix in the spices and garlic. Rub the spiced butter all over the cauliflower and season well. Bring the sides of the foil up and wrap round the cauliflower, then bake in the oven for 20 minutes.

3. To make the dressing, put the raisins into a small bowl and cover with very hot water. Set aside for 30 minutes, then drain, retaining some of the soaking liquid. Rinse the capers very well in cold water. Heat the olive oil in a small pan, add the drained raisins and the capers and cook quickly for a few minutes. Add the sherry vinegar, parsley and a little of the soaking liquid and season well.

4. After the cauliflower has been in the oven for 20 minutes, take it out and fold back the foil round the sides. Baste the cauli with the melted butter in the bottom of the foil, then return it to the oven for another 10–15 minutes, or until tender.

5. To serve, place the whole cauliflower in a serving dish and pour the dressing over the top.

I first came across cooking a cauliflower whole when I had lunch at Bob's (see page 149). It is based on a dish served by Rene Redzepi of Noma restaurant in Copenhagen. Redzepi roasts his cauli whole with butter and branches of pine, spruce and juniper, then finishes it by mixing the buttery juices with apple vinegar and yoghurt whey. To serve, he tops the cauli with horseradish cream.

JANE

# Addie May's Christmas Nut Loaf

SERVES 4 • PREPARATION TIME: 15 MINUTES • COOKING TIME: 45 MINUTES • V Ⓥ

We could not put together a vegetarian cookbook and leave out the nut loaf. This is a celebratory version, and is quite easy to make.

1 tablespoon **olive oil**

1 **onion**, chopped

1 **red pepper**, deseeded and chopped

2 cloves of **garlic**, crushed

220g **mixed nuts**, chopped (we used **pecans**, **walnuts** and **cashews**)

50g **ground almonds**

75g **chestnut purée**

50g soft **breadcrumbs**

2 **eggs**

100ml **milk**

100g cooked **spinach**, chopped

**salt** and **freshly ground black pepper**

100g **cranberry sauce**

125g **blue cheese**, crumbled

1. Heat the oven to 200°C/400°F/gas mark 6.

2. Heat the oil in a frying pan, add the onion, red pepper and garlic, and cook for 5 minutes, until soft. Transfer to a large bowl and add the mixed nuts, ground almonds, chestnut purée and breadcrumbs.

3. Whisk together the eggs and milk and stir into the nut mixture, along with the chopped spinach. Season well.

4. Line a loaf or terrine tin with baking parchment. Spread half the nut and vegetable mixture along the bottom, then top with the cranberry sauce and sprinkle with the crumbled blue cheese. Finish with the rest of the nut and vegetable mix.

5. Bake in the oven for 40 minutes. Allow to cool slightly, then turn out on to a serving plate.

**TIPS**

* Freshen it up with chopped fresh herbs.

* Some sage leaves, fried in butter until crisp, would make a great addition, sprinkled over the top before serving.

Addie May came to the Field Kitchen for a week's work experience when she was fifteen, and was there in various capacities on and off for the next six years. She is an immensely talented cook and a very hard worker who would on many occasions be seen whizzing around the kitchen in a 'cloud' of flour, making nine puddings before eleven o'clock in the morning. This is her grandmother's recipe, which she cooks for herself every Christmas, being the only vegetarian in her immediate family. Addie is currently studying medicine, with the hope of working for Médecins Sans Frontières.

JANE

ADDIE MAY, CHAPEL STREET, HALIFAX, 1981

# Stuffed Vegetables

SERVES 4 • PREPARATION TIME: 15 MINUTES • COOKING TIME: 10 MINUTES • ♥ ✓ WF GF DF V

There are many versions and ways of stuffing vegetables. The stuffing below is one we all like – it suits various vegetables and methods. Old-fashioned but very good.

**vegetables of your choice**
(see method)

### FOR THE STUFFING

1 tablespoon **olive oil**

1 **red onion**, finely chopped

1 tablespoon **balsamic vinegar**

50g **raisins**, soaked in very
hot water

200g **cooked rice**

75g **pine nuts**, toasted

1 x 300g tin of **chickpeas**,
drained and rinsed

100g cooked **spinach**, chopped

2 large **tomatoes**, chopped

1 tablespoon chopped
**fresh flat-leaf parsley**

1 tablespoon chopped
**fresh mint** (or dill)

a pinch of **ground allspice**

a pinch of **cayenne pepper**

75g **feta** or **goat's cheese**
(optional), crumbled

**salt** and **freshly ground
black pepper**

### PREPARING THE STUFFING

1. Heat the oil in a pan, add the onion and cook over a medium heat for 5 minutes. Add the balsamic vinegar and cook for another 2 minutes, then tip into a large bowl.

2. Squeeze out the raisins and add to the onion along with the rice and toasted pine nuts.

3. Mash half the chickpeas and add to the bowl with the remaining chickpeas, left whole. Stir in the spinach and the rest of the ingredients and season very well. Your stuffing is now ready to go.

### STUFFING & COOKING VEGETABLES

**Aubergines:** Cut in half lengthways and slash the flesh with a knife. Place on a baking tray, rub with olive oil and cook in a preheated oven at 160°C/325°F/gas mark 3 for 10 minutes. Scoop out some of the cooked flesh, chop and add to the stuffing ingredients. Stuff the aubergines, then bake for a further 20 minutes.

**Butternut squash, or other small squash:** Cut the squash in half lengthways and scoop out and discard the seeds and pith. Brush the cut surfaces with olive oil, place on a baking tray and cook in a preheated oven at 200°C/400°F/gas mark 6 for 30 minutes, or until the flesh is tender. Remove from the oven and reduce the oven temperature to 160°C/325°F/gas mark 3. Scoop out some of the cooked flesh, chop, and add to the stuffing ingredients. Season well, then return the mixture to the skins and cook for a further 15 minutes.

**Courgettes**: Cut in half lengthways and scoop out the centre with a teaspoon. Stuff, then place on a baking tray and cook in a preheated oven at 160°C/325°F/gas mark 3 for 20 minutes.

**Greens**: Blanch cabbage leaves or tender spring green leaves in a pan of boiling water for just a few minutes. Drain, refresh under cold water, drain again then allow to cool. Place the leaves flat on a work surface. Place a little stuffing in the centre of each leaf and roll up into a parcel. Pack the parcels together in an oiled baking dish, brush with olive oil, then cover and cook in a preheated oven at 150°C/300°F/gas mark 2 for 10–15 minutes.

**Onions**: Peel the onions and cook in a pan of boiling salted water for 10 minutes, then drain. Trim the stem end and spoon out the centre, leaving a shell. Roughly chop the centre flesh, mix with the stuffing mixture and season well. Stuff the mixture back into the onion shells and brush all over with olive oil. Place on a baking tray and cook in a preheated oven at 160°C/325°F/gas mark 3 for 20 minutes.

**Peppers**: Halve and deseed. Stuff the halves and place on a baking tray. Cook in a preheated oven at 160°C/325°F/gas mark 3 for 20 minutes, then serve.

**Tomatoes**: Slice off the stem end and scoop out the pulp (this can be set aside and used in another dish). Stuff with the stuffing mixture, place on a baking tray and cook in a preheated oven at 160°C/325°F/gas mark 3 for 20 minutes.

BRUNO & HIS FAMILY, 1969

My first job was as a commis chef for Bruno Loubet at the Four Seasons, Inn on The Park in London. Despite holding a Michelin star he would recklessly put dishes on the menu that his gran had cooked for him. I loved him for it. Stuffed vegetables were one of his favourites. Simple, unpretentious, stylish in an old-school way and very, very good.

HENRY

VEGETABLES PRIOR TO COOKING

# RICE & CURRY

LEON

# Green Bean & Cashew Curry

SERVES 4 • PREPARATION TIME: 10 MINUTES • COOKING TIME: 20 MINUTES • ♥ ✓ WF GF DF V

Fresh cashew nuts are often used in curries throughout India and Africa. If you are lucky enough to have some to hand, increase the cooking time to 30 minutes in step 1 before adding the French beans. Unsalted cashews are widely available and can be used in this recipe.

1 **onion**, thinly sliced

2 **red chillies**, deseeded and sliced crossways

2 cloves of **garlic**, crushed

a 2cm piece of **fresh ginger**, grated

2 strips of **lemon rind**

¼ teaspoon **ground turmeric**

a 4cm stick of **cinnamon**

10 **curry leaves** (dried ones are fine)

100g **cashew nuts** (unsalted)

1 x 440ml tin of **coconut milk**

250g **French beans**, trimmed and halved

**salt**

1. Place all the ingredients apart from the French beans and salt in a pan and bring to a simmer, then continue to cook for about 10 minutes over a low heat.

2. Add the French beans and stir well, then continue to simmer for another 10 minutes, or until the beans are tender, stirring occasionally.

3. Season well with salt, then serve.

**TIPS**

* Chopped coriander may be added before serving.

* You can use salted cashews, but make sure to soak them in hot water for 30 minutes before starting the recipe.

* Runner beans and/or sugar snap peas make a nice substitute for the French beans.

* The sauce can be used to cook all sorts of vegetables, so experiment to create your own trademark vegetable curry.

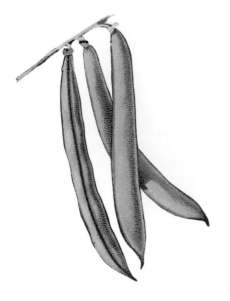

# Pilau with Cashews & Raisins

SERVES 4–6 • PREPARATION TIME: 10 MINUTES • COOKING TIME: 20 MINUTES • ♥ ✓ WF GF DF V

Another great cashew dish. This aromatic rice dish can stand on its own or be served as part of a banquet (see page 292).

400g **basmati rice**

2 tablespoons **sunflower oil**

1 **cinnamon stick**

4 **cloves**

2 **cardamom pods**

2 **bay leaves**

4 cloves of **garlic**, crushed

a 4cm piece of **ginger**, grated

2 **onions**, chopped

4 **green chillies**

**salt** and **freshly ground black pepper**

250g **frozen peas**

1 litre **vegetable stock** or **water**

100g **unsalted cashews**

100g **raisins**

1 tablespoon chopped **fresh mint** and **coriander**

1. Put the rice into a bowl, cover it with cold water, and leave to soak for 30 minutes.

2. Heat 1 tablespoon of the oil in a large pan, then add the cinnamon, cloves, cardamom and bay leaves and cook over a medium heat for 3 minutes.

3. Blend the garlic and ginger with 3 tablespoons of water to make a paste and add to the spices in the pan. Cook for another few minutes, without browning the garlic.

4. Add the onions, chillies and a little salt and cook over a low heat for 5 minutes.

5. Drain the rice well and add it to the onion mixture along with the peas. Cook for a minute, then add the vegetable stock or water. Bring to a simmer, then cover the pan and cook very slowly for 5–10 minutes, or until the rice is tender.

6. While the rice is cooking, heat the remaining tablespoon of oil in a frying pan and fry the nuts and raisins for a few minutes, or until the nuts just start turning golden. Add them to the cooked rice along with the herbs, season well, then serve.

**TIPS**

* Try adding a few sultanas or flaked almonds to this dish before serving.

* Broad beans, chopped sugar snap peas or beans can be added alongside the peas if you like.

* Dotting over a few cubes of butter and a squeeze of lemon to the cooked rice will add extra flavour.

# Stuffed Aubergine Curry

SERVES 4 • PREPARATION TIME: 15 MINUTES • COOKING TIME: 25 MINUTES • ♥ ✓ WF GF DF V

Small aubergines are best suited to this recipe; however, the large ones will work too (you may have to lengthen the cooking time).

6–8 **small aubergines**
(about 700g)

2 tablespoons **sunflower oil**

100ml **water**

**salt** and **freshly ground black pepper**

**FOR THE STUFFING**

30g **sesame seeds**

75g **unsalted roasted peanuts**

2 tablespoons **maple syrup**

1 teaspoon **salt**

½ teaspoon **ground turmeric**

½ teaspoon **cayenne pepper**

1 clove of **garlic**, crushed

1 tablespoon chopped **fresh coriander**

1. Put all the stuffing ingredients into a food processor with a little water and blitz together to make a paste.

2. Cut each aubergine in half lengthways, but do not cut through the stem. Roll the aubergine over and cut again so that it is quartered but is still intact at the stem.

3. Divide the stuffing between the aubergines, using a teaspoon to spread it over the inside cut surfaces. Squeeze the quarters back together.

4. Heat the oil in a large frying pan with a lid (one that will hold all the aubergines in one layer). Add the aubergines to the pan and cook over a medium heat for 5 minutes, turning them occasionally to brown them all over.

5. Add the water, then cover the pan and simmer over a low heat for 20 minutes, turning halfway through, until the aubergines are tender. Season and serve.

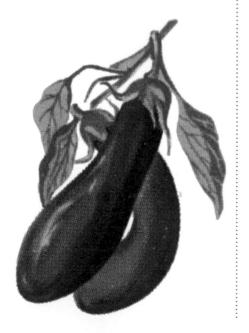

**VARIATIONS**

✿ Try substituting the aubergines for courgettes.

# Grated Beetroot Curry

SERVES 4 • PREPARATION TIME: 10 MINUTES • COOKING TIME: 20 MINUTES • ♥ ✓ WF GF DF V

Lots of beetroot curries are coconut-based, but not this one. It is very dry and has nutty gram flour (besan) added towards the end of the cooking time.

3 large **beetroot**

2 tablespoons **sunflower oil**

½ tablespoon **mustard seeds**

½ tablespoon **cumin seeds**

1 **onion**, sliced

2 cloves of **garlic**, crushed

1 **red or green chilli**, chopped

10 **curry leaves**

**salt** and **freshly ground black pepper**

1 tablespoon **gram flour**

a pinch of **ground turmeric**

1. Peel and coarsely grate the beetroot.

2. Heat the oil in a large frying pan and cook the mustard and cumin seeds over a medium heat for a few minutes, or until they start to pop.

3. Quickly add the onion, garlic, chillies and curry leaves and season well with salt.

4. Cook for 2 minutes, then stir in the grated beetroot and cook for a further 10 minutes over a medium heat.

5. Sprinkle over the gram flour, turmeric and 2 tablespoons of water. Stir well, then cover the pan and simmer over a low heat for 5 minutes. Season and serve.

JANE AND DAVID (WITH BUNSKY) AT ANNIE'S FLAT, LONDON, 2003

**BY AIRMAIL**
**PAR AVION**

Sri Lankan cooking is primarily vegetable-based, but the veg served vary depending on the region you are visiting. I visited last year with my son David. We initially headed inland to the hill country and its tea plantations. It was colder and damper than we expected, and we were not prepared for a climate in which hot water bottles were the norm at bedtime. We spotted trucks carrying bunched carrots, beetroot and even turnips, completely different from the long beans, bitter gourds and okra grown around the tropical, coastal lowlands. The vegetables grown at altitude suit the climate and were brought here by the English, along with the Hill Club and red postboxes.

JANE

# Stir-fried Spiced Spring Greens

SERVES 4 • PREPARATION TIME: 10 MINUTES • COOKING TIME: 12 MINUTES • ♥ ✓ WF DF V

Spring greens are abundant during the spring and early summer before summer greens become available. A great side dish for any curry.

500g **spring (or summer) greens**

1 heaped tablespoon **desiccated coconut**

¼ teaspoon **ground turmeric**

¼ teaspoon **chilli powder**

1 tablespoon **olive oil**

1 **onion**, finely chopped

1 teaspoon mixed **cumin** and **mustard seeds**

1 **dried chilli**, crushed

a 2cm piece of **fresh ginger**, grated

1 clove of **garlic**, crushed

**salt** and **freshly ground black pepper**

a squeeze of **lime juice**, to taste

1. Roll up the spring greens tightly and shred them finely across, down to the thick base stalks. Place them in a colander and wash well with cold water.

2. Put the coconut into a small bowl and add 1 tablespoon of boiling water. Sprinkle in the turmeric and chilli powder and stir well. Set aside.

3. Heat the oil in a wok or a large frying pan, then add the onion and cook over a medium heat for 5 minutes. Add the cumin and mustard seeds, chilli, ginger and garlic and cook for another 2 minutes.

4. Add the shredded greens and a little salt, mix well, then turn up the heat, stirring vigorously for about 5 minutes, until the greens are wilted. If they start to stick to the pan, add a little water.

5. Finally, stir in the coconut mixture and lime juice, season, then serve.

**VARIATIONS**

✿ Savoy, Hispi and January King cabbages can all be used as an alternative to spring greens.

✿ Cauliflower florets can also be braised with the spice mix and cooked in the same way as the cabbage, although they may need to be cooked for a little longer and in a covered pan.

✿ Add a tin of chickpeas or black-eyed beans to the greens to turn the dish into something more substantial.

# Tandoori Cauliflower

SERVES 4 • PREPARATION TIME: 5 MINUTES • COOKING TIME: 25 MINUTES • ♥ ✓ WF GF V

To stay ahead of the game, you can prepare the first two steps of this recipe the day before. The cauliflower will also have extra marinating time.

1 large **cauliflower**, cut into florets

**FOR THE PASTE**

2 tablespoons ready-made **tandoori paste** (or see Tips)

150ml **natural yoghurt**

1 clove of **garlic**, crushed

a 4cm piece of **fresh ginger**, grated

1 **red chilli**, chopped

1 tablespoon chopped **fresh coriander**

**salt** and **freshly ground black pepper**

1. Mix together all the paste ingredients in a bowl and season well.

2. Bring a large pan of salted water to the boil. Add the cauliflower florets and blanch for 3 minutes, then refresh in cold water and drain. Put the cauliflower into a bowl, add the paste, and set aside to marinate for at least 15 minutes.

3. When ready to cook, heat the oven to 180°C/350°F/gas mark 4. Put the cauliflower into a roasting tray and pop it into the oven for 15–20 minutes, or until it is tender.

**TIPS**

* The recipe above uses a ready-made tandoori paste, but if you have the time and all the following spices to hand you can easily make your own:

**HOMEMADE TANDOORI PASTE**

1 teaspoon **ground turmeric**
3 cloves of **garlic**, crushed
1 tablespoon **fresh ginger**, grated
2 tablespoons **lime juice**
1 teaspoon **chilli powder**
2 teaspoons **paprika**
½ teaspoon **ground cumin**
1 tablespoon **garam masala**
1 teaspoon **salt**

Blend all the spices together to form a paste, then use in the recipe above.

# Dhal

SERVES 4 • PREPARATION TIME: 15 MINUTES • COOKING TIME: 45 MINUTES • ♥ ✓ WF GF DF V

A very simple dhal recipe. It can be used as the base for a more substantial meal by serving it with a fried or poached egg on top and rice alongside.

150g **split yellow peas** (**chana dhal**), soaked overnight in cold water

500ml **water**

**salt** and **freshly ground black pepper**

1 tablespoon **sunflower oil**

1 tablespoon **mustard seeds**

½ tablespoon **cumin seeds**

a pinch of **ground turmeric**

10 **curry leaves**

1 **onion**, sliced

5 **green chillie**s, sliced

3 cloves of **garlic**, crushed

1 teaspoon **garam masala**

3 large **tomatoes**, chopped

**TO SERVE (OPTIONAL)**

juice of ½ a **lemon**

chopped **fresh coriander**

1. Drain the soaked split peas, then rinse and place in a large pan. Pour over the 500ml of water, bring to the boil, then reduce the heat and simmer for about 30 minutes, or until the peas are very soft. Season well.

2. Heat the oil in a large pan. Add the spices and curry leaves and fry over a medium heat until the mustard seeds start to pop.

3. Quickly add the onion, chillies and garlic and stir well. Cook for another 3 minutes, then add the garam masala.

4. Mix well, then tip in the cooked dhal and the tomatoes. Bring to a simmer and cook for a further 10 minutes, adding more water if the mixture becomes too thick. Season well.

**TIPS**

* To finish, you can add a little lemon juice and chopped coriander.

* Cooked vegetables such as cauliflower florets and French beans can be added to the dhal at the end, for more texture and flavour.

# Pineapple Curry

SERVES 4 • PREPARATION TIME: 15 MINUTES • COOKING TIME: 15 MINUTES • ♥ WF GF DF V

This is a traditional Sri Lankan dish and is found all over the island.

1 **fresh pineapple**

1 tablespoon **sunflower oil**

1 **onion**, finely chopped

1 **yellow pepper**, diced

1 stick of **cinnamon**

10 **curry leaves**

1 teaspoon **mustard seeds**

3 cloves of **garlic**, crushed

a 2cm piece of **fresh ginger**, grated

1 **red chilli**, chopped

1 teaspoon **curry powder**

¼ teaspoon **ground turmeric**

**salt**

125ml **coconut milk**

1. Remove the tough skin from the pineapple and chop the flesh into small rough chunks. Set aside.

2. Heat the oil in a large pan and add the onion, yellow pepper, cinnamon, curry leaves and mustard seeds. Cook for 2 minutes over a medium heat.

3. Add the garlic, ginger, chilli and spices, stir well, and cook for another 2 minutes. Season with salt.

4. Tip in the pineapple chunks and coconut milk, stir, then bring to a simmer over a low heat. Continue to simmer for another 10 minutes, then check the seasoning and serve.

POLLUVIL MARKET, SRI LANKA

**TIPS**

* Make sure your pineapple is on the firm side of ripe. It needs to retain its astringency or this dish can get sickly sweet.

# Squash, Corn & Bean Stew

SERVES 4 • PREPARATION TIME: 15 MINUTES • COOKING TIME: 30 MINUTES • ♥ WF GF DF V

The stuff of bonfires and chilly evenings. This can be let down with a little vegetable stock and turned into a soup. It's great with tortilla chips sprinkled on top.

2 tablespoons **olive oil**

2 medium **onions**, chopped

1 **red pepper**, chopped

3 cloves of **garlic**, crushed

1 teaspoon **ground cumin**

2 teaspoons **ground paprika**

2 **corn cobs**, kernels removed

400g **butternut squash**, peeled and cut into small dice

4 large **tomatoes**, roughly chopped

**salt** and **freshly ground black pepper**

250ml **vegetable stock**

1 x 440 tin of **pinto beans** (or **borlotti** or **cannellini beans**), drained

1. Heat the oil in a large saucepan over a medium heat. Add the onions, red pepper and garlic and cook for 5 minutes.

2. Add the spices, corn kernels, squash and tomatoes and mix well. Cook for another 5 minutes, stirring to make sure the vegetables doesn't stick to the pan. Season well.

3. Add the stock and bring to a simmer, then cover the pan and cook gently over a low heat for 20 minutes, or until the squash is tender. (Add more stock or water if required.)

4. Stir in the drained beans and warm through. Season well and serve.

**TIPS**

* We have used butternut squash which is easy to prepare, but other squashes and pumpkins work well.

* The stew can be garnished with fresh coriander, parsley or chives.

* Try adding a chopped fresh red chilli in step 1 if you like it hot.

**THREE SISTERS STEW**

The Native Americans referred to squash, corn and beans as the 'three sisters' because the three vegetables grow together harmoniously. Bean seeds would be sown at the base of the corn with the squash sown in between – the corn would grow quickly so that the beans (which provided nitrogen in the soil for the other two) could grow up it. The squash would grow at ground level and surpress any weeds and keep the soil moist – they could all be harvested at the same time.

# Mushroom Mapo Tofu

SERVES 4 • PREPARATION TIME: 10 MINUTES • COOKING TIME: 15 MINUTES • ♥ ✓ WF GF DF V

A classic, very spicy Chinese dish that is usually made with minced meat and tofu, but this vegan version still delivers the punch that is associated with the original.

1 tablespoon **sunflower oil**

½ teaspoon **ground Szechuan pepper**

1 teaspoon **dried chilli flakes**

5 cloves of **garlic**, crushed

a 5 cm piece of **fresh ginger**, finely grated

250g **mushrooms**, sliced

2 tablespoons **chilli bean paste**

1 tablespoon **soy sauce**

2 teaspoons **balsamic vinegar**

400g firm **tofu**, cut into 1–2cm cubes

**salt** and **freshly ground black pepper**

1 teaspoon **toasted sesame oil**

a bunch of **spring onions**, finely sliced

1. Heat the oil in a wok over a high heat and add the Szechuan pepper, quickly followed by the chilli flakes, garlic and ginger, stirring constantly and moving the ingredients around the pan.

2. Turn the heat down to medium, add the mushrooms, bean paste, soy sauce and vinegar and simmer for 5 minutes, stirring occasionally.

3. Now add the tofu cubes, mix well and cook over a low heat for another 5 minutes. Check the seasoning, then finish with a little toasted sesame oil and sprinkle with sliced spring onions. Serve with plain steamed rice.

**VARIATIONS**

✿ For a more authentic taste, substitute tiny dried whole chillies for the chilli flakes.

✿ Diced aubergines can be used instead of mushrooms, as they are perfect for absorbing the spicy sauce.

# Sri Lankan Milk Rice

SERVES 4 • PREPARATION TIME: 5 MINUTES • COOKING TIME: 25 MINUTES • WF GF DF V

Traditionally this is served on feast days in Sri Lanka – especially on New Year's Day – and is usually cut into diamond shapes. It is equally good accompanying sweet or savoury dishes. Try serving it with a fiery *sambool* (a Sri Lankan condiment) or with palm sugar and bananas.

420g **short-grain rice**

750ml **water**

500ml **coconut milk**

1 teaspoon **salt**

1 **cinnamon stick**

2 **cardamom pods**

1. Wash the rice in cold water and drain. Place in a pan with the water and bring to the boil, then reduce the heat to low and simmer for 15 minutes.

2. Add the coconut milk, salt and spices. Stir, then cover the pan and continue to simmer for a further 10 minutes (or until all the coconut milk has been absorbed).

3. Allow to cool slightly, then turn the rice out into a shallow tray lined with greaseproof paper. Press the rice down into the tray.

4. Cut into diamond shapes and serve.

> In Sri Lanka, the array of vegetables and local fruit used is wonderfully imaginative, though you might not guess it from the menus advertising 'rice and curry'. In general this is made up of one small meat or fish dish and five, or even six, vegetable dishes with rice. Every cook has their own very distinctive vegetable curry recipe and it's a great way of making sure the vegetables are the star of the dish. JANE

# Henry's Basic Basmati Rice

PREPARATION TIME: NONE • COOKING TIME: 25 MINUTES • WF GF DF V

For every 1 cup of **rice**, add 1¼ cups of **water**

1. Melt a little butter or oil in a large saucepan.

2. Stir in the rice and cook gently for 2 minutes before adding the water.

3. Bring to the boil, then cover the pan and reduce the heat to the very lowest setting. It will be ready in 20 minutes.

**TIPS**

* For a better finish, rinse your rice in a sieve under cold running water before cooking. Make sure you drain it well before proceeding.

* By adding a knob more butter at the start and cooking over a medium heat for 5 minutes at the end, you get delicious crispy bits that you can scrape off the bottom and stir through the rice. Be careful not to burn it, though.

* Try adding a pinch of saffron (or turmeric) and some whole spices such as cardamom and cinnamon to the oil and butter, cooking them gently before adding the rice.

# PART TWO

## SUPPORTING CAST

LEON

◆〈 **FULL OF SUN** 〉◆

Grazing dishes, sides, relishes
& puddings

# GRAZING DISHES & SIDES

LEON

# Dressings, Sauces, etc.

One of the simplest ways to add zip to cooked vegetables or pulses is to dress them. These are some of our favourite dressings and things to serve with them.

## Salpicón Dressing

SERVES 4 • PREPARATION TIME: 15 MINUTES
COOKING TIME: NONE • ♥ WF GF DF V

'Salpicón' generally means 'chopped up', and is used to describe many Mexican and South American dishes. Our version is inspired by Mark Miller's Coyote Café and has a refreshing New Mexico slant.

½ a **red pepper**, finely diced

½ a **yellow pepper**, finely diced

3 **shallots** (or 1 **red onion**), finely chopped

1 clove of **garlic**, crushed

1 **red chilli**, finely chopped

1 tablespoon **rice vinegar**

1 tablespoon **lime juice**

2 tablespoons **groundnut oil**

1 teaspoon **caster sugar** (or **honey**)

1 tablespoon chopped **mixed fresh herbs** (e.g. parsley, chives)

**salt** and **freshly ground black pepper**

1. Put all the ingredients into a bowl and whisk together. Season well, then set aside so that the flavours can develop.

2. After 30 minutes, the dressing is ready to use.

### Things to sauce with salpicón:

• Simply toss with avocado.

• Mix into warm new potatoes to make a colourful potato salad.

• Create a salad of toasted tortilla strips, watercress, corn and avocado.

• Use to dress quinoa or couscous.

• Pour over grilled leeks and cauliflower florets.

## Larb Dressing

SERVES 4 • PREPARATION TIME: 10 MINUTES
COOKING TIME: 5 MINUTES • ♥ WF GF DF V

This Thai salad dressing is normally used with finely chopped meat. The ground toasted rice gives it its unique texture and flavour.

1 heaped tablespoon uncooked **fragrant Jasmine rice** or **sticky rice**

½ **red onion**, finely chopped

2 **red chillies**, finely chopped

2 tablespoons **light soy sauce**

4 tablespoons **lime juice**

a pinch of **soft brown sugar**

1 tablespoon chopped **lemongrass**

1 tablespoon chopped **fresh mint** and **coriander**

a pinch of **cayenne pepper**

1. Dry-roast the rice in a non-stick frying pan until golden in colour. Allow to cool, then grind to a rough powder in a spice grinder or using a pestle and mortar.

2. Put the rest of the ingredients into a bowl and mix together. Check that the balance is right between sweet, salty and sour and that there is enough heat there.

3. Toss your vegetables in the dressing and sprinkle with the toasted ground rice.

### Very fresh crisp vegetables are best with larb, such as:

• Wedges of Little Gem or other similar lettuce.

• Cucumber, radishes, red peppers, tomatoes.

• Blanched French and runner beans/ sugar snap peas/mangetout/asparagus/ broccoli/cauliflower.

• Cooked greens.

# Devilled Sauce

MAKES ENOUGH TO DRIZZLE OVER 4 SERVINGS OF VEG
PREPARATION TIME: 5 MINUTES
COOKING TIME: 10 MINUTES • ✓ WF GF V

This cream-based sauce can be used with any vegetables. Add more mustard, Tabasco or garlic to suit your palate.

25g **butter**

1 tablespoon **olive oil**

1 large **shallot**, finely chopped

2 cloves of **garlic**, crushed

50ml **white wine**

150ml **double cream**

2 teaspoons **English mustard powder**

2 teaspoons **Dijon mustard**

2 teaspoons **tomato purée**

1 teaspoon **ground black pepper**

a dash of **Worcestershire sauce**

a dash of **Tabasco**

1 teaspoon **maple syrup**

**salt**

chopped **chives** or **parsley** (optional)

1. Melt the butter with the oil in a small pan and cook the shallot over a medium heat for 5 minutes. Add the garlic and stir well. Cook for a minute, then add the wine, turn up the heat and simmer until the wine has reduced by half.

2. Add the rest of the ingredients, whisk together, then cook over a medium heat for 5 minutes. Check the seasoning and add extra Tabasco, etc., if required.

3. Your sauce is now ready to use. Below are some serving suggestions, but we feel it would work with most veg.

**Some things that devil well:**
- Cooked new potatoes.
- Halved soft-boiled eggs.
- French and runner beans.
- Sweetcorn, peppers and courgettes.
- Cabbage and white beans.

# Seaweed Butter

SERVES 4 • PREPARATION TIME: 5 MINUTES
COOKING TIME: 5 MINUTES • ✓ WF GF V

This butter can be used with any vegetable, particularly asparagus, broccoli and cauliflower. Toss the cooked vegetables in the butter and season.

50g **butter**

1 tablespoon **nori flakes** or chopped **nori sheets**

juice of 1 **lemon**

**salt** and **freshly ground black pepper**

1. Heat half the butter in a small pan until it begins to brown – it will start to froth. Remove the pan from the heat when the froth clears.

2. Quickly add the nori flakes or chopped nori and the rest of the butter. Stir well. Add the lemon juice, whisk together and season well.

# Pink Peppercorn & Elderflower Dressing

SERVES 4–6 • PREPARATION TIME: 5 MINUTES
COOKING TIME: NONE • WF GF V

This is based on a dressing made by the great Joyce Molyneux, mentor to Jane, who cooked at the Carved Angel in Dartmouth, Devon. It is good with salads containing avocado, asparagus or even strawberries. It is equally delicious with simple, crisp lettuce.

1 tablespoon **pink peppercorns**

1½ tablespoons **white wine vinegar**

2 teaspoons **elderflower cordial**

75ml **groundnut oil**

75ml **single cream**

1 tablespoon chopped **fresh chives**

**salt** and **freshly ground black pepper**

1. Grind the pink peppercorns roughly either in a spice grinder or using a pestle and mortar.

2. Place in a liquidizer with the rest of the ingredients and blend together until an emulsion is formed. Season well.

# Griddled Hispi Cabbage

## WITH A CHILLI & MINT DRESSING

SERVES 4 • PREPARATION TIME: 10 MINUTES • COOKING TIME: 10 MINUTES • ♥ WF GF DF V

Here's a different way to cook cabbage. You want it to retain some crunch. It is important to place the hot grilled hispi straight into the dressing for maximum flavour.

1 **hispi cabbage** (or other pointed cabbage)

1 tablespoon **olive oil**

### FOR THE CHILLI & MINT DRESSING

3 tablespoons **olive oil**

1 tablespoon **red wine vinegar**

1 **red chilli**, chopped

2 teaspoons **honey**

1 clove of **garlic**, crushed

1 tablespoon chopped **fresh mint**

**salt** and **freshly ground black pepper**

1. Put all the dressing ingredients into a bowl and whisk together. Pour into a shallow, wide container.

2. Peel off any sad-looking outer leaves from the cabbage and trim the base slightly, leaving the leaves intact and still attached. Cut the cabbage in half lengthways, then again, to give you quarters.

3. Cut each cabbage quarter into thin wedges and toss them in a little oil.

4. Heat a griddle pan and grill the pieces of cabbage, turning them over when charred lines appear. While still hot, place the cabbage in the dressing. You will have to do this in batches, turning the cabbage in the dressing after each addition.

5. Check the seasoning and serve.

### TIPS

* Tossing your grilled or roasted vegetables straight into a dressing while still hot really helps develop the flavours of the dish.

# Truffled Cabbage & Leeks

SERVES 6 • PREPARATION TIME: 10 MINUTES • COOKING TIME: 15 MINUTES • ✓ WF GF V

Cooking vegetables in the oven improves their flavour. The natural juices, mixed with the cheese and truffle oil, make a dish that may not make it to the table! If you are lucky enough to have some truffle paste, stir a little through the mixture.

1 small **Savoy cabbage**

3 **leeks**

30g **butter**, melted

1 tablespoon **olive oil**

**salt** and **freshly ground black pepper**

50ml **water**

1 tablespoon grated **fontina** or **Gruyère cheese**

a good drizzle of **truffle oil**

1. Heat the oven to 200°C/400°F/gas mark 6.

2. Strip away any damaged leaves from the cabbage and cut it in half. Cut each half into thin wedges. Trim the leeks and slice across (1cm thick) on the diagonal.

3. Spread the vegetables in a large oven tray. Mix with the melted butter and olive oil and season well. Pour over the water and cover tightly with kitchen foil. Cook in the oven for about 15 minutes, or until the cabbage core is tender.

4. Transfer to a serving dish, sprinkle with the cheese, then drizzle with truffle oil and serve.

**TIPS**

* Cauliflower and broccoli can be cooked in the same way. They cook surprisingly quickly and the flavour is far better than when boiled.

* Try this with other cabbage varieties.

* Delicious with goat's cheese sprinkled on top.

# Broccoli with Miso Butter Sauce

SERVES 4 • PREPARATION TIME: 10 MINUTES • COOKING TIME: 5 MINUTES • WF GF V

This is a great sauce that can be used with lots of other vegetables.

30g **butter**

1 bunch of **spring onions**, chopped

2 tablespoons **rice vinegar**

1 tablespoon chopped **fresh ginger**

1 tablespoon **red miso**

2 teaspoons **soy sauce**

400g **broccoli**

**salt** and **freshly ground black pepper**

1 tablespoon chopped **fresh coriander**

1. Melt the butter in a pan and whisk in the onions, vinegar, ginger, red miso and soy sauce. Cook over a low heat for 2 minutes, then set aside.

2. Cut the broccoli into florets, then peel the stalk and cut it into batons. Cook the broccoli in a large pan of boiling salted water for 3 minutes. Drain well.

3. Tip the broccoli into the butter sauce, stir in the coriander, season well and serve.

**TIPS**

* Try this sauce with other veg, such as cauliflower; new potatoes; kale; purple sprouting broccoli or romanesco.

# Leeks Vinaigrette

SERVES 4 • PREPARATION TIME: 5 MINUTES • COOKING TIME: 5 MINUTES • ♥ ✓ WF GF DF V

The leeks in this recipe can either be cooked in boiling salted water or blanched and grilled. We have suggested a couple of different dressings below, which can also be used with other grilled vegetables.

6–8 **leeks**

**salt** and **freshly ground black pepper**

1 tablespoon **olive oil**

**··· TIPS ···**

* This can also be served with Basil Dressing (see page 69) or Red Pepper & Almond Dressing (see page 224).

1. Trim the leeks and cut each one down the middle lengthways to 2cm above the root, but without cutting it in half. Wash them well in cold water and drain.

2. Bring a pan of salted water to the boil, add the leeks and cook them for 5 minutes, until just tender. Drain well, split each leek in half, then toss them in the oil and season well.

3. At this point the leeks can either be dressed with one of the dressings below, or grilled on a preheated griddle pan (or a barbecue) and then dressed. For maximum flavour, dress the leeks while still warm or hot.

## Hazelnut Dressing

SERVES 4–6 • PREPARATION TIME: 10 MINUTES
COOKING TIME: NONE • ✓ WF GF DF V

4 tablespoons **olive oil**

¼ of a **red onion**, finely chopped

2 tablespoons **balsamic vinegar**

1 tablespoon chopped **fresh parsley**

2 teaspoons chopped **fresh tarragon**

2 tablespoons roasted, skinned and chopped **hazelnuts**

1 clove of **garlic**, crushed

1. Put all the ingredients into a bowl and whisk together.

2. Drizzle over the leeks.

## Egg & Mustard Dressing

SERVES 4–6 • PREPARATION TIME: 5 MINUTES
COOKING TIME: NONE • ✓ WF GF DF V

2 tablespoons **olive oil**

1 tablespoon **white wine vinegar**

1 tablespoon **coarse-grain mustard**

2 teaspoons **honey**

1 tablespoon chopped **fresh parsley**

**salt** and **freshly ground black pepper**

2 hard-boiled **eggs**, chopped

1. Put the oil, vinegar, mustard, honey and parsley into a bowl and mix together. Season well.

2. Drizzle over the leeks and sprinkle with the chopped egg.

# Turnips, Beetroot & Orange

SERVES 4 • PREPARATION TIME: 10 MINUTES • COOKING TIME: 30 MINUTES • ♥ WF DF V

Marmalade makes a great addition to lots of savoury dishes and works especially well with beetroot.

400g **turnips**, peeled

400g **beetroot**, peeled

2 tablespoons **olive oil**

**salt** and **freshly ground black pepper**

1 tablespoon **marmalade**

100ml **orange juice**

2 tablespoons **balsamic vinegar**

1 tablespoon **butter**

1 tablespoon chopped **fresh flat-leaf parsley**

**chopped walnuts** (optional)

1. Heat the oven to 170°C/325°F/gas mark 3. Chop the turnips and beetroot into 2cm dice or wedges. Toss in the olive oil, season, then roast in the oven for 30 minutes, or until tender.

2. Put the marmalade into a large pan with the orange juice, vinegar and butter and heat gently. Tip in the roasted vegetables and turn up the heat. Cook, stirring, until the vegetables are glazed, then remove from the heat and season. Scatter over the parsley and the walnuts (if using) and serve.

**T I P S**

* Dry-fry some caraway seeds and add them with the marmalade for an aniseedy kick.

# Carrots with Ginger & Honey

SERVES 6 • PREPARATION TIME: 10 MINUTES • COOKING TIME: 30 MINUTES • WF DF V

Cooking carrots this way enhances their flavour and produces a lovely glaze. It's best to use a large pan so that the carrots cook evenly and there is less chance of the pan catching.

500g **carrots**

30g **butter**

1 tablespoon **honey**

2cm piece of **fresh ginger**, peeled and grated

**salt** and **freshly ground black pepper**

juice of ½ a **lemon**

1 tablespoon chopped **fresh coriander**

1. Prepare the carrots. If they are small and young, leave them whole and unpeeled. Larger carrots can be peeled and cut into 2–3cm chunks.

2. Place the carrots in a large pan with the butter, honey and ginger. Cook over a high heat for 2–3 minutes, stirring continuously. Season well, then cover, turn the heat down to low and cook for 10–15 minutes, or until the carrots are tender.

3. Remove the lid, turn up the heat and add the lemon juice. Cook for 1 minute, until the carrots have a glazed appearance. Check the seasoning, scatter over the coriander and serve.

**VARIATIONS**

❧ Try this with turnip chunks, using 1 tablespoon each of butter, vinegar and parsley.

❧ Try it with beetroot using 1 tablespoon each of butter, orange juice and balsamic vinegar.

# Smashed Pea Bruschetta

SERVES 6 • PREPARATION TIME: 10 MINUTES • COOKING TIME: 5 MINUTES • V

If you can't get good-quality fresh peas (which are fairly hard to find unless you are growing your own), frozen peas are fine – they should not be destined to be just another vegetable in a roast dinner.

250g **peas**

2 cloves of **garlic**, one crushed and one left whole

grated zest of ½ a **lemon**

50g **pecorino cheese** (or **vegetarian Parmesan-style cheese**)

250g **ricotta cheese**

2 tablespoons **olive oil**, plus more to drizzle

**salt** and **freshly ground black pepper**

6 slices of **sourdough or ciabatta bread**

1. Bring a pan of salted water to the boil. Add the peas and cook for 2 minutes, then drain and set aside to cool until warm.

2. Put the peas into a bowl. Add the crushed garlic clove, lemon zest, pecorino, ricotta and olive oil and mix well.

3. Take out half the mixture and blitz roughly in a blender, then put back into the bowl and fold into the rest of the mixture. Season well.

4. Preheat the grill or a griddle pan and toast the bread on both sides. Cut the whole garlic clove in half and rub the toasted bread with it, then drizzle with olive oil.

5. Top the bruschetta with a generous amount of the pea mixture and serve.

**TIPS**

* Smashed cooked broad beans with a little oil and pecorino also makes a great bruschetta topping.

* When making bruschetta, never oil the bread first – grill the bread dry, rub with a garlic clove, then drizzle with good-quality extra virgin olive oil.

# Smoky Braised Romaine

SERVES 4 • PREPARATION TIME: 10 MINUTES • COOKING TIME: 20 MINUTES • ♥ ✓ WF GF DF V

The chipotle sauce gives a deliciously smoky flavour to this dish, but if you find it hard to come by, try using a smoky barbecue sauce.

2 heads of **Romaine lettuce**

1 tablespoon **olive oil**

½ a **red onion**, finely chopped

½ a **red pepper**, finely chopped

1 clove of **garlic**, crushed

1 tablespoon **black mustard seeds**

2 teaspoons **chipotle sauce**

**salt** and **freshly ground black pepper**

1. Cut the Romaine lettuce lengthways into 6 wedges.

2. Heat the oil in a large shallow pan in which the wedges will fit tightly, and brown the cut sides of the lettuce over a medium heat. Remove from the pan and set aside.

3. Add the onion and pepper to the pan and cook gently for 5 minutes.

4. Add the garlic and mustard seeds and turn up the heat under the pan, frying for a minute until the seeds begin to pop. Remove from the heat.

5. Stir in the chipotle sauce and return the lettuce wedges to the pan along with any juices, turning the lettuce in the sauce.

6. Cover the pan and cook gently over a low heat for 10 minutes. Season and serve.

**VARIATIONS**

❀ Try this dish with heads of Little Gem as they are a variety of lettuce that taste great when cooked.

❀ Instead of the spices and smoky sauce, try adding peas and fresh mint to the braised lettuce.

❀ Radicchio also gives great results when cooked – braise it with a little garlic, a splash of balsamic vinegar and a sprig of chopped marjoram.

# Corn Fritters

## WITH CHUNKY GUACAMOLE

SERVES 6 • PREPARATION TIME: 10 MINUTES • COOKING TIME: 10 MINUTES • ♥ WF GF V

These fritters are always popular at parties, with a dollop of guacamole.

3 cobs of **sweetcorn**, cooked

2 **eggs**

1 **egg yolk**

125ml **milk**

2 tablespoons **rice flour**

2 tablespoons **gram flour**

1 tablespoon **polenta**

1 teaspoon **bicarbonate of soda**

1 **red onion**, finely chopped

1 **red chilli**, finely chopped (optional)

1 clove of **garlic**, crushed

1 teaspoon **sesame oil**

**salt** and **freshly ground black pepper**

**olive oil** or **butter**, for frying

1. Remove the kernels from the sweetcorn cobs by standing them upright on a chopping board and cutting downwards with a sawing action.

2. Put the eggs, egg yolk and milk into a bowl and whisk together.

3. Sift the flours, polenta and bicarbonate of soda into a large bowl. Slowly pour in the egg mixture, whisking until you have a smooth batter.

4. Add the rest of the ingredients, apart from the oil or butter for frying, then stir in the corn kernels and season well.

5. Heat a tablespoon of olive oil or butter in a non-stick frying pan and drop spoonfuls of batter into the pan, making small rounds. Cook them for 2 minutes on each side over a medium heat. This can be done in batches. Remove the fritters from the pan and serve with Chunky Guacamole (see below).

## TIPS

* Replace the milk with soya milk to make the fritters totally dairy free.

* The fritters take on a nutty flavour when fried in butter.

* Guacamole is good served as a dip with tortilla chips or spread on toast.

## Chunky Guacamole

SERVES 6 • PREPARATION TIME: 15 MINUTES
COOKING TIME: NONE • ♥ WF GF V

2 ripe **avocados**, roughly chopped

½ a **red onion**, finely chopped

1 tablespoon chopped **fresh coriander**

1 clove of **garlic**, crushed

juice of 1 **lime**

2 **tomatoes**, finely chopped

1 **red chilli**, finely chopped

1 tablespoon **olive oil**

**salt** and **freshly ground black pepper**

1. Put all the ingredients into a bowl.

2. Mix together and season well, then serve immediately.

# Madeira Mushrooms on Toast

SERVES 2–4 • PREPARATION TIME: 10 MINUTES • COOKING TIME: 10 MINUTES • V Ⓥ

Here is a basic snack given the royal treatment with the addition of Madeira and cream. A large variety of mushrooms are now available – so (if possible) use a mixture of field, chestnut and others as well as the usual button mushrooms.

1 tablespoon **butter**

1 tablespoon **olive oil**

2 **shallots**, chopped

1 clove of **garlic**, crushed

1 teaspoon **fresh thyme leaves**

400g **mushrooms**, sliced

100ml **Madeira**

100ml **double cream**

**salt** and **freshly ground black pepper**

1 tablespoon chopped **fresh flat-leaf parsley**

4 slices of **sourdough or ciabatta bread**

1. Melt the butter with the oil in a large shallow frying pan, then add the shallots and cook over a medium heat for 3 minutes.

2. Add the garlic and thyme leaves, mix well, then tip in the mushrooms. Turn up the heat and stir for a few minutes until they have softened.

3. Add the Madeira and continue to cook over a high heat for 2 minutes, stirring well. Add the cream, then turn down the heat and simmer for a few minutes, until the sauce has reduced and is coating the mushrooms. Season, and stir in some of the parsley.

4. Preheat the grill or a griddle pan and toast the bread on both sides. Place in a serving dish, top with the mushrooms and scatter over the remaining parsley.

**TIPS**

* Button mushrooms are fantastic and much underrated as a vegetable – use them with pride.

**VARIATIONS**

❀ For something more rustic use a mixture of field and chestnut mushrooms.

❀ Or try adding a few soaked and chopped dry porcini and use their soaking liquor to make the sauce by reducing it for a stronger flavour.

GRAZING DISHES & SIDES  **211**

# Squash & Tomatoes

SERVES 4 • PREPARATION TIME: 10 MINUTES • COOKING TIME: 30 MINUTES • ♥ ✓ WF GF DF V

A great side, with the squash working surprisingly well alongside the tomatoes and basil.

1 tablespoon **olive oil**

1 **onion**, chopped

400g **butternut squash**
(or other squash)

**salt** and **freshly ground
black pepper**

2 cloves of **garlic**, crushed

250g **cherry tomatoes**, halved

a small bunch of **fresh basil**,
leaves shredded

1 tablespoon **balsamic vinegar**

25g **butter**

1. Heat the oil in a large shallow pan and cook the onion for 5 minutes over a medium heat.

2. While the onion is cooking, peel the squash, remove the seeds and cut the flesh into 1cm dice. Add to the onion and mix well, then season and cook over a medium heat until the squash is soft. Cover the pan to speed up the cooking. You should get nice brown caramelized bits.

3. Stir in the garlic and cook for a minute longer, then tip in the tomatoes and cook for 5 minutes more. Add the basil, vinegar and butter. Mix well, season well and serve.

# Pumpkin, Leeks & Sage

SERVES 4 • PREPARATION TIME: 15 MINUTES • COOKING TIME: 20 MINUTES • ♥ ✓ WF GF V

500g **pumpkin flesh**, peeled

2 tablespoons **olive oil**

**salt** and **freshly ground
black pepper**

1 **red onion**, sliced

5 **fresh sage leaves**, shredded

4 **leeks**, sliced across finely

1 tablespoon **balsamic vinegar**

slivers of **vegetarian
Parmesan-style cheese**, to
serve (optional)

1. Preheat the grill or a griddle pan. Slice the pumpkin finely, then put into a bowl and toss with half the olive oil. Season well, then grill for a few minutes on each side.

2. While the pumpkin is grilling, heat the rest of the oil in a large pan. Cook the onion with the sage leaves for 5 minutes over a medium heat. Season, then add the leeks and cook for a further 5 minutes, stirring well. Stir in the balsamic vinegar and remove from the heat.

3. Arrange the pumpkin slices in a large serving dish and top with the onion and leeks. You can also add some Parmesan slivers, if you like.

# Sweet Potatoes with Garlic, Ginger & Coriander

SERVES 4 • PREPARATION TIME: 15 MINUTES • COOKING TIME: 15 MINUTES • ♥ ✓ WF GF DF V

Simple, pretty, healthy and delicious.

500g **sweet potatoes**

4–5 large cloves of **garlic**

a 5–6cm piece of **fresh ginger**

stalks and a few leaves from 1 small bunch of **fresh coriander**

4 tablespoons **sunflower oil**

2 level teaspoons **chilli flakes** (without seeds) or 1 teaspoon **chilli powder**

**sea salt**

1–2 tablespoons **extra virgin olive oil**

1. Peel the sweet potatoes, cut them in half lengthways, then slice 1cm thick.

2. Peel the garlic and ginger and chop together finely.

3. Cut off the very base of the coriander stalks and discard, then chop the stalks roughly, together with a few of the leaves.

4. Bring a pan of water to the boil and steam the sweet potatoes until they are tender right through when you insert a small knife (but don't leave them so long that they start to break up).

5. While the sweet potatoes are steaming, put the sunflower oil into a largish sauté pan over a low heat. Add the chopped garlic and ginger and stir until translucent and just beginning to brown in places, then remove from the heat.

6. When the sweet potatoes are cooked, add them to the garlic and ginger. Add the chopped coriander, the chilli flakes and a sprinkling of sea salt and stir over the heat for another minute or two. Remove from the heat, stir in the extra virgin olive oil and serve.

**TIPS**

* Steaming root vegetables is a healthy way of cooking them. They cook a lot quicker than you think they will.

* Try substituting butternut squash or pumpkin for the sweet potato.

MOLLY, LIZA, EMMA, JOSSY, KATE, HENRY AND ANNA, 1976

# Braised Swede & Celery

SERVES 6 • PREPARATION TIME: 10 MINUTES • COOKING TIME: 20 MINUTES • ♥ ✓ WF GF V

Two under-used vegetables that deserve more respect.

25g **butter**

1 tablespoon **olive oil**

1 **onion**, chopped

1 clove of **garlic**, crushed

**salt** and **freshly ground black pepper**

400g **swede**

2 **celery hearts**

1 teaspoon **fresh thyme leaves**

100ml **white wine**

1 teaspoon **Marmite**

100ml **water**

1 tablespoon **soy sauce**

1. Melt the butter with the oil in a large pan, add the onion, garlic and a little salt and cook for 3 minutes over a medium heat.

2. Peel the swede and cut it into 1cm dice. Cut the celery into chunks roughly the same size as the swede. Add to the pan of onions, along with the thyme leaves.

3. Turn the heat up to high and cook for about 1 minute, stirring continuously. Add the wine, Marmite, water and soy sauce. Mix well and bring up to a simmer, then cover and cook for about 15 minutes, or until the swede is tender. Season with lots of black pepper and serve.

# Swede, Apricots & Ginger

SERVES 4 • PREPARATION TIME: 10 MINUTES • COOKING TIME: 30 MINUTES • ♥ WF GF DF V

A warming dish for the bleak mid-winter.

1 tablespoon **olive oil**

1 **onion**, chopped

2 teaspoons grated **fresh ginger**

50g **dried apricots**, chopped

1 tablespoon **honey**

50g **butter**

100ml **white wine**

500g **swede**, peeled and cut into fine batons

**salt** and **freshly ground black pepper**

1. Heat the oven to 160°C/325°F/gas mark 3.

2. Heat the oil in a large pan, then add the onion and ginger and cook over a medium heat for 5 minutes.

3. Add the apricots, honey, butter and white wine to the pan, then add the swede. Turn up the heat, season and cook over a high heat for 5 minutes, stirring well.

4. Transfer everything to an ovenproof dish and cover with foil. Bake in the oven for 20 minutes, or until the swede is tender.

When I started writing this book. I was determined to eat only British, seasonal vegetables produced without the use of a hothouse for a whole year. Riverford Farm kindly offered to send me such a veg box. I started well on a wave of late summer abundance and I was still going strong as the orange colours of autumn arrived. By early February, I am ashamed to say, I had given up broken by a relentless assault of kale and swede. This was one of my many swede experiments I completed before I cracked. HENRY

# Shredded Sprouts

SERVES 4 • PREPARATION TIME: 10 MINUTES • COOKING TIME: 15 MINUTES • ♥ ✓ WF GF V

Sprouts are like baby cabbages and can be sliced and cooked like cabbage in many ways.

400g **Brussels sprouts**

1 tablespoon **olive oil**

1 tablespoon **butter**

2 teaspoons **caraway seeds**

1 clove of **garlic**, crushed

**salt** and **freshly ground black pepper**

1 tablespoon **balsamic vinegar**

juice and grated zest of 1 **orange**

1. Finely shred the sprouts.

2. Heat the oil with the butter in a large shallow pan, then add the caraway seeds and fry over a medium heat until they start to pop. Quickly add the garlic, stir well and tip in the shredded sprouts. Cook over a medium heat for 5 minutes and season well.

3. Add the vinegar, orange juice and zest and cook for a further 5 minutes, then serve.

# Sprouts with Honey & Capers

SERVES 4 • PREPARATION TIME: 5 MINUTES • COOKING TIME: 15 MINUTES • ♥ WF GF V

Roasting sprouts intensifies their flavour. There is no smell that hangs around like a boiled sprout.

400g **Brussels sprouts**

1 tablespoon **olive oil**

2 teaspoons **honey**

2 tablespoons **capers**, soaked in plenty of cold water and squeezed out

**salt** and **freshly ground black pepper**

50g **vegetarian Parmesan-style cheese**, grated

1. Heat the oven to 160°C/325°F/gas mark 3.

2. Peel away the outer leaves from the sprouts and discard. Cut the sprouts in half and put them into a baking tray. Toss them with the olive oil and roast in the oven for 10 minutes.

3. Remove the sprouts from the oven and drizzle them with the honey. Sprinkle over the capers, mix well and return to the oven for a further 5 minutes.

4. Put the sprouts into a serving dish and season well. Top with the Parmesan and serve.

**TIPS**

* Shredded sprouts can be used in most recipes that ask for shredded cabbage or spring greens.

* For extra flavour, roast the sprouts with a little honey and balsamic vinegar and sprinkle with toasted pine nuts.

# Aubergines with a Miso Glaze

SERVES 4 • PREPARATION TIME: 10 MINUTES • COOKING TIME: 20 MINUTES • ♥ WF GF DF V

There are many versions of this dish. It is one of the tastiest ways to serve aubergines.

2 large **aubergines**
(or 4 small ones)

1 tablespoon **olive oil**

3 tablespoons **miso paste**

2 tablespoons **mirin**
(or **sweet rice wine**)

1 tablespoon **sake**
(or **dry sherry**)

1 tablespoon **sugar**

1 teaspoon **sesame oil**

1 tablespoon **sesame seeds**

a bunch of **spring onions**,
finely sliced

1. Heat the oven to 180°C/350°F/gas mark 4 and line a baking tray with baking parchment.

2. Cut the aubergines across into discs about 3cm thick and score the cut surface in a criss-cross fashion with a knife. Brush both sides of the slices with oil and place on the prepared baking tray. Bake in the oven for 15 minutes, until the aubergines are tender.

3. Put the miso paste, mirin, sake, sugar and sesame oil into a bowl and mix together.

4. Spread some of the miso mixture over each slice of aubergine and sprinkle with the sesame seeds. Flash under a hot grill until bubbling on top.

5. Transfer the aubergines to a serving dish and sprinkle with the spring onions.

# Aubergine Involtini

SERVES 4 • PREPARATION TIME: 20 MINUTES • COOKING TIME: 20 MINUTES • WF GF V

These can also be made with grilled courgettes. You could also try rolling the two together.

2 **aubergines**

1 tablespoon **olive oil**

**salt** and **freshly ground black pepper**

150g **ricotta cheese**

150g **mozzarella cheese**

1 **egg yolk**

2 tablespoons grated **vegetarian Parmesan-style cheese**

100g **piquillo peppers** (or other peeled **red peppers**), chopped

a small bunch of **fresh basil**, leaves shredded

3 tablespoons **Tomato Sauce** (see page 145)

1. Heat the oven to 160°C/325°/gas mark 3. Slice the aubergines lengthways into thin strips (about 0.5cm wide). Put them into a bowl, toss them with the olive oil and season well.

2. Heat a griddle pan and grill the aubergine strips for 2 minutes on each side, until slightly browned and tender.

3. Put the ricotta, mozzarella, egg yolk and half the Parmesan into a bowl and mix together. Stir in the chopped peppers and basil and season well.

4. Lay the aubergine strips out on a work surface and spread each one with a teaspoon of Tomato Sauce. Put a dessertspoon of the cheese mixture at one end and roll up the aubergine strip. Repeat this with the rest of the aubergine.

5. Place the parcels in an ovenproof dish into which they all fit snugly.

6. Sprinkle with the rest of the Parmesan, bake in the oven for 15 minutes, then serve.

CAULIFLOWER & LEEKS WITH RED PEPPER & ALMOND DRESSING

CAULIFLOWER AS COUSCOUS

# Cauliflower & Leeks

## WITH RED PEPPER & ALMOND DRESSING

SERVES 4 • PREPARATION TIME: 15 MINUTES • COOKING TIME: 25 MINUTES • ♥ WF GF DF V

We've used cauliflower and leeks here (see page 222), but the dressing is also great with French and runner beans, broccoli/purple sprouting or mixed roast roots.

1 **cauliflower**, broken into florets

½ teaspoon **smoked paprika**

4 tablespoons **olive oil**

**salt** and **freshly ground black pepper**

4 **leeks**

100g **piquillo peppers** (or other peeled red peppers), chopped

70g **almonds**, toasted

1 tablespoon **balsamic vinegar**

1 tablespoon **honey**

1 tablespoon chopped **chives**

1. Heat the oven to 180°C/350°F/gas mark 4. Put the cauliflower florets into a bowl and toss with the smoked paprika and 1 tablespoon of the olive oil. Season well, then transfer to a baking tray and put into the oven for 15–20 minutes, until golden brown and tender.

2. Wash and trim the leeks, then cut them in half lengthways down as far as the root but without cutting through it. Bring a large pan of salted water to the boil, then add the leeks and blanch for 5 minutes. Drain and pat dry. Toss in a little more of the olive oil and season.

3. Heat a griddle pan over a high heat (or use a barbecue). Split the leeks in half and grill for a minute on each side. Cut each half across into 2cm pieces and keep them warm.

4. Put the remaining olive oil into a serving bowl with the rest of the ingredients and whisk together to make the dressing, seasoning well.

5. When the cauli comes out of the oven, add it to the bowl and toss it with the dressing, then fold in the leeks. Season well and serve.

**TIPS**

* It's fine to roast the leeks instead of grilling them.

* Try adding halved roasted sprouts (a good use of Christmas leftovers).

# Cauliflower as Couscous

SERVES 4 • PREPARATION TIME: 10 MINUTES • COOKING TIME: 5 MINUTES • ♥ WF GF DF V

Breaking down the cauliflower florets gives them a texture like couscous, and they only need brief cooking. Use as you would couscous, as a salad, a side or a hot accompaniment (see page 223).

1 **cauliflower**

1 tablespoon **olive oil**

a pinch of **curry powder**

1 tablespoon **white wine vinegar**

1 tablespoon **maple syrup**

**salt** and **freshly ground black pepper**

1 **apple**, finely chopped

1 bunch of **spring onions**, finely chopped

1 tablespoon chopped **fresh mint**

1 tablespoon chopped **fresh coriander**

1. Core the cauliflower and divide it into florets. Chop finely, either by hand or in a food processor.

2. Heat the oil in a large shallow frying pan or wok. Add the curry powder and stir quickly, then add the cauliflower, vinegar and maple syrup. Season well. Stir quickly over a medium heat for 5 minutes, or until the cauliflower is just tender.

3. Remove from the heat and add the rest of the ingredients. This can be served either hot or at room temperature.

**TIPS**

* Pine nuts or almonds could be added, along with chopped red peppers and crumbled feta cheese.

* For a different dish, try chopped cooked plain cauliflower with fresh chives, grated vegetarian Parmesan-style cheese and truffle oil.

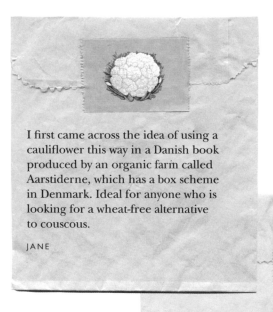

I first came across the idea of using a cauliflower this way in a Danish book produced by an organic farm called Aarstiderne, which has a box scheme in Denmark. Ideal for anyone who is looking for a wheat-free alternative to couscous.

JANE

This dish is a marvel. It really does eat like couscous, but with better flavour and without the heaviness. There is a touch to Jane's cooking that often takes dishes to a higher level. That touch is evident here.

HENRY

# Jerusalem Artichokes & Shallots

## WITH HAZELNUT AILLADE

SERVES 4 • PREPARATION TIME: 15 MINUTES • COOKING TIME: 30 MINUTES • ♥ ✓ WF GF DF V

Pounding the nuts and garlic together makes a thick, punchy dressing. Walnuts can be substituted, and the dressing can be used with a variety of other roast vegetables.

600g **Jerusalem artichokes**, peeled

200g **shallots**, peeled

1 tablespoon **olive oil**

**salt** and **freshly ground black pepper**

1 tablespoon **balsamic vinegar**

100g **watercress**

1 tablespoon chopped **fresh flat-leaf parsley**

**lemon wedges**, to serve

**FOR THE HAZELNUT AILLADE**

50g **hazelnuts**, roasted and peeled

2 cloves of **garlic**, crushed

70ml **olive oil**

grated zest of 1 **orange**

1. Heat the oven to 180°C/350°F/gas mark 4.

2. Put the artichokes and shallots into a bowl and toss with the olive oil, then season well and place on a baking tray. Roast for 30 minutes, or until tender, then remove from the oven and drizzle with the vinegar.

3. While the vegetables are roasting, make the aillade by blitzing the nuts and garlic together in a food processor until roughly chopped. Slowly add the olive oil to make a thick emulsion, then mix in the orange zest and season well.

4. Place the roast vegetables on a serving dish with a large bunch of watercress to the side and a dollop of aillade. Sprinkle with the parsley and serve with a lemon wedge.

## TIPS

* If the Jerusalem artichokes are clean and not too knobbly, it may not be necessary to peel them – just wash them very well and give them a good scrub.

* If you can seek out large banana shallots and use them instead of the diddy ones. It makes peeling and prep much easier.

# Kale Crisps

SERVES 4 • PREPARATION TIME: 10 MINUTES • COOKING TIME: 15 MINUTES • ♥ ✓ WF GF DF V

Cavolo nero or black kale gives the best results here. Red Russian and curly kale can be used too, but may need a shorter cooking time.

1 bunch of **kale** (300g)

1 tablespoon **olive oil**

**salt**

**lemon juice**

1. Heat the oven to 180°C/350°F/gas mark 4.

2. Wash the kale well and strip the leaves from the central stems. Dry the leaves between tea towels or using a salad spinner.

3. Toss the kale in the olive oil and place on a baking tray. Roast in the oven for about 15 minutes, until crisp.

4. Remove from the oven and sprinkle with salt and a squeeze of lemon.

## TIPS

* It's important to keep checking your kale while it's in the oven and moving the leaves around – ovens rarely have a constant temperature throughout and you can be left with leaves that are soggy in some places and burned in others.

# Spinach & Sesame Balls

MAKES 12 SMALL BALLS • PREPARATION TIME: 5 MINUTES • COOKING TIME: 3 MINUTES • ♥ ✓ WF GF DF V

These are simple to make and are good to serve with drinks.

350g **spinach**

1 tablespoon **sesame seeds**

1 teaspoon **miso paste**

**salt** and **freshly ground black pepper**

1 teaspoon **wasabi paste**, to taste

1 tablespoon **soy sauce**, to taste

1. Remove any thick stalks from the spinach and discard. Wash the spinach leaves well and drain.

2. Bring a large pan of salted water to the boil, then add the spinach and cook very briefly for about 30 seconds. Drain and refresh under cold water, then squeeze out any excess moisture. Put the spinach into a bowl.

3. Put the sesame seeds into a small frying pan over a medium heat and dry-fry until brown and toasted. Add to the spinach, then stir in the miso paste. Season well.

4. Combine the wasabi with the soy sauce and pour into a dipping bowl.

5. Roll the spinach mixture into small balls and serve with cocktail sticks and the dipping sauce.

# Sambal French & Runner Beans with Tempeh

A powerful, fresh and zesty curry. Indonesian sambal dishes usually contain the pungent *blachan* (shrimp paste) and dried shrimps. However, sambal olek chilli paste and tamarind are now widely available and work well as substitutes.

150g **French beans**

150g **runner beans**

1 tablespoon **sunflower oil**

1 **onion**, finely chopped

2 cloves of **garlic**, crushed

120g **tempeh**, thinly sliced

3 teaspoons **sambal oelek**

½ teaspoon **tamarind paste**

a pinch of **sugar**

3 tablespoons hot **water**

**salt** and **freshly ground black pepper**

1. Top and tail the French beans. String the runner beans and thinly slice them diagonally.

2. Heat the oil in a shallow frying pan, then add the onion and cook over a medium heat for 5 minutes. Add the garlic, mix well and cook for a few more minutes. Add the tempeh and turn up the heat to brown it for a few minutes.

3. Quickly add the rest of the ingredients, including the beans and water. Stir well and continue to cook over a high heat for 5 minutes.

4. Cover the pan, then turn the heat to low and leave to simmer for a further 5 minutes. The beans should be tender and coated with the sauce. Season well and serve.

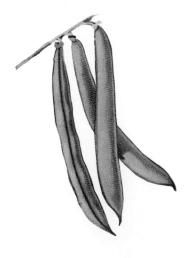

**TIPS**

* Finish with lots of fresh coriander and chopped spring onions.

**VARIATIONS**

✿ Fried tofu cubes could be added instead of the tempeh.

✿ You can substitute the vegetables with cauliflower, broccoli or anything you happen to have about.

# Celeriac, Leeks & Chard

SERVES 4 • PREPARATION TIME: 15 MINUTES • COOKING TIME: 20 MINUTES • ♥ ✓ WF GF DF V

To make this dish well, care needs to be taken to make sure that all three vegetable components are cooked and well seasoned. After that it is basically an assembly job.

1 tablespoon **sultanas**

100ml **boiling water**

1 small **celeriac** (about 300g)

2 tablespoons **olive oil**

**salt** and **freshly ground black pepper**

a pinch of **saffron threads**

100ml **vegetable stock** or **water**

4 **leeks**, sliced into 1cm discs

150g **chard leaves**, washed

1 tablespoon **toasted pine nuts**

a pinch of **sumac**

1. Heat the oven to 200°C/400°F/gas mark 6. Put the sultanas into a bowl, pour over the boiling water and set aside to soak.

2. Peel the celeriac, then cut it in half and cut each half into thin slices. Toss the slices in 1 tablespoon of olive oil. Season and spread out on a baking tray. Place in the oven for about 20 minutes, or until the celeriac is tender.

3. While the celeriac is cooking, put the remaining tablespoon of oil in a wide shallow pan with the saffron and vegetable stock. Bring to the boil, then reduce the heat to low and simmer for 5 minutes.

4. Add the sliced leeks to the liquid, season, then cover the pan and continue to simmer for a further 5 minutes, or until the leeks are tender.

5. Bring a large pan of salted water to the boil, then add the chard leaves and blanch briefly. Drain, refresh under running cold water and squeeze out any excess moisture with your hands. Chop the chard roughly and sprinkle over the leeks to warm through.

6. Drain the soaked sultanas well, then start to assemble the dish on a large serving plate. Spread half the celeriac pieces over the plate, followed by half the leek and chard mixture, then sprinkle with half the sultanas and pine nuts. Repeat with the rest of the ingredients, finishing with a dusting of sumac.

# Quick-fried Celeriac with Apples & Walnuts

SERVES 6 • PREPARATION TIME: 10 MINUTES • COOKING TIME: 10 MINUTES • ♥ ✓ WF GF DF V

This is a light way to cook root vegetables. The thinner you cut the batons, the more quickly they will be ready.

1 small **celeriac**

2 tablespoons **olive oil**

**salt** and **freshly ground black pepper**

2 **apples**, cored and diced

70g **walnuts**, chopped

a pinch of **cayenne pepper**

2 teaspoons **cider vinegar**

1 tablespoon chopped **fresh chives**

1.  Peel the celeriac and cut into fine batons. This is easily done by first cutting the peeled celeriac into slices and then cutting each one into thin matchsticks.

2.  Heat the oil in a large shallow pan and cook the celeriac over a medium heat for about 10 minutes, stirring continuously until the root is tender. Season well.

3.  Remove from the heat, stir in the rest of the ingredients and serve.

## TIPS

* To improve the flavour of walnuts (or pecans), sprinkle them with salt and cayenne and roast them in a hot oven for a few minutes. This will remove any stale taste and give them extra oomph.

* Parsnips could be substituted for the celeriac, and so could any other root vegetable, although cooking times may vary.

* You can prepare the celeriac using the grater attachment of a food processor.

# Polenta with Creamed Kale

SERVES 4 • PREPARATION TIME: 5 MINUTES • COOKING TIME: 50 MINUTES • WF GF V

We tend to use black kale (cavolo nero) for this recipe, but it works just as well with curly and red Russian varieties of kale. This is a versatile dish (see Tips below).

400g **kale**

1 tablespoon **olive oil**

2 cloves of **garlic**, crushed

1 **dried chilli**, crumbled

**salt** and **freshly ground black pepper**

200ml **double cream**

1 tablespoon **vegetarian Parmesan-style cheese**, to serve

**TO SERVE**

750ml **water**

**salt**

125g **polenta**

1. First make the polenta. Bring the water to the boil and add a little salt. Slowly add the polenta, whisking as you pour it in. Reduce the heat and simmer gently for 40 minutes, whisking now and again. Pour into a greased baking tray 1–2cm deep and leave to cool. When cool, cut into wedges and grill on a hot griddle for a few minutes on each side. Keep warm while you make the creamed kale.

2. Wash the kale in lots of cold water. Strip the leaves from the central rib. Discard the rib and drain the leaves.

3. Bring a large pan of salted water to the boil, add the kale leaves and blanch them for 3 minutes, or until tender. Drain, then refresh under cold water and squeeze out any excess moisture. Chop the kale roughly.

4. Heat the oil in a shallow pan over a medium heat, then add the garlic and chilli and stir for a minute. Add the chopped kale, season well and cook for 2 minutes stirring occasionally.

5. Add the cream, then turn up the heat and simmer for 2 minutes. The cream should coat the kale.

6. Remove half the mixture and blend in a food processor or blender, then stir it back into the mixture in the pan. Season well and serve sprinkled with Parmesan.

**TIPS**

* This makes a good pasta sauce for penne or Fresh Orecchiette (see page 144).

* Try it mixed into wet polenta as an alternative to colcannon.

**VARIATIONS**

✿ You can leave out the cream and add olive oil to make a lighter option for a pasta sauce, or to serve on bruschetta.

✿ Add an egg yolk and bake in the oven, either in a gratin dish or in a tart shell.

# Mashed Potato

This is a simple classic mash the way we like to make it – with no surprises, and it works well. However, we have followed it with some variations that are definitely worth the extra effort.

1kg **floury potatoes**
(bakers are good)

**salt** and **freshly ground black pepper**

100ml **milk**

100ml **double cream**

75g **butter**

**MASH KEY**

MUSTARD MASH

SAFFRON MASH

SPRING ONION & CHIVE MASH

PLAIN MASH

RED PEPPER MASH

MARMITE & CHEESE MASH

CREAMED KALE MASH

CABBAGE MASH

SWEET POTATO MASH

1. Peel the potatoes, cut them into large chunks and place them in a large pan. Cover with water, season with salt and bring to the boil.

2. Reduce the heat and simmer for 15 minutes, or until the potatoes are just tender. Drain in a colander, then set aside, covered with a tea towel, for a few minutes.

3. Meanwhile, put the milk, cream and butter into the pan and cook over a low heat until the butter has melted and the mixture is hot. Season.

4. Place a mouli-légumes (food mill) over the pan of hot cream and pass the potatoes through the fine blade into the pan. A potato ricer also gives good results.

5. Beat the potatoes into the cream mixture, then check the seasoning and serve.

**VARIATIONS**

✿ Add a good pinch of saffron threads to the potato cooking water, then pass the potatoes through a mouli and pour in some good olive oil. Beat with an electric mixer until fluffy.

✿ Add both Dijon and wholegrain mustard to your finished mash.

✿ Cook lots of shredded cabbage in butter and add to the finished mash.

✿ Finely chop 3 bunches of spring onions and add to the finished mash with lots of chopped chives.

✿ Add Creamed Kale (see page 234) to the finished mash.

✿ Try it 50:50 mash and another mashed root, such as celeriac or Jerusalem artichokes.

✿ Mash roast sweet potatoes with wasabi paste to taste.

✿ Blend piquillo peppers (or other peeled red peppers) with chilli, garlic and olive oil, then add to the cooked mashed potato.

✿ For a garlic mash, add peeled garlic cloves to the potatoes while they're cooking in the boiling water and pass them through a food mill or potato ricer with the potatoes. For an extra dimension, roast whole heads of garlic in the oven until soft and squeeze out the creamy insides of the cloves into the cooked mash.

✿ Add squeezy Marmite to taste and some grated cheese to the finished mash.

# Roast Mixed Roots

SERVES 4 • PREPARATION TIME: 10 MINUTES • COOKING TIME: 40 MINUTES • WF GF DF V

When roasting roots some vegetables will take longer than others to cook, so careful monitoring is required. However, if you are cooking a large quantity, it is preferable to roast each vegetable separately and mix them together at the end when each is cooked to perfection.

1kg **mixed root vegetables** (e.g. carrots, celeriac, parsnips, beetroots, turnips)

8 cloves of **garlic**

1 teaspoon **fresh thyme leaves**

2 tablespoons **olive oil**

**salt** and **freshly ground black pepper**

1. Heat the oven to 160°C/325°F/gas mark 3. Peel the root vegetables and cut them into 2–3cm chunks or wedges.

2. Place the vegetables in a large roasting tray with the garlic and thyme leaves and drizzle with olive oil. Season, then toss everything with your hands.

3. Roast in the oven for about 20 minutes, then check, shake the pan and turn the vegetables over using a palette knife. Put back into the oven for a further 20 minutes, or until tender.

## VARIATIONS

❀ Peel and halve parsnips and place in a roasting tray. Drizzle with mustard and maple syrup and dot with butter, then roast in the oven for 30 minutes.

❀ Put squash pieces in a roasting tray, toss in olive oil and roast in the oven. When almost cooked, sprinkle with chopped fresh rosemary, finely chopped fresh red chilli and finely chopped garlic. Return to the oven and roast for a further 5 minutes.

❀ Roast turnip halves in the oven sprinkled with brown sugar, vinegar and dotted with butter. Finish scattered with chopped fresh parsley.

❀ Roast carrots (whole if possible) tossed in olive oil and a sprinkling of ground cumin, then serve with crumbled feta on top and chopped fresh mint.

❀ Parboil potato wedges in water infused with saffron. Roast in the oven tossed in olive oil, crushed garlic and bay leaves. Scatter with crushed almonds to finish.

❀ Slice red onions and cook them slowly in a little butter and olive oil in a pan over a low heat for 15 minutes, without browning. Roast the potatoes in the oven for 20 minutes, then add the cooked onions, a knob of butter and 1 tablespoon of balsamic vinegar. Mix well then roast for a further 20 minutes, or until the potatoes are cooked.

❀ Parboil halved potatoes in boiling salted water for 6 minutes, then drain. Meanwhile, slice an onion and cook in a pan with a little olive oil for 5 minutes. Combine the potatoes and cooked onions in a baking dish and toss in olive oil, peeled cloves of garlic and chopped semi-dried tomatoes. Roast in the oven until cooked and finish scattered with shredded fresh basil leaves.

❀ Roast potato wedges in a large roasting tray for 20 minutes. Meanwhile, slice the fennel into 1cm wedges and braise in olive oil over a low heat for 15 minutes. Add to the potatoes with chopped fresh rosemary and roast in the oven until cooked.

# Roast Potatoes

Everybody loves a good roast potato, but people often fret over the process required to perfect them. For the best results it is important to use a suitable variety of spud, and after parboiling create a rough surface on the spud before placing in hot oil.

1kg **potatoes** (King Edward, Desiree or Maris Piper are best), peeled and halved

**salt** and **freshly ground black pepper**

3 tablespoons **olive oil**

### TIPS

* When draining the parboiled potatoes, allow them to dry out for a few minutes covered with a clean tea towel – this will help absorb excess moisture and dry them out to make them even crispier.

1.  Heat the oven to 200°C/400°F/gas mark 6.

2.  Place the potatoes in a pan and cover with cold water, then add a teaspoon of salt and bring to the boil. Reduce the heat and simmer the potatoes for 6 minutes, then drain well. Return them to the pan, put the lid on, and shake well to rough up the edges of the potatoes.

3.  Meanwhile, pour the oil into a roasting tray and place in the oven.

4.  When the potatoes are ready, remove the roasting tray from the oven and place on the hob over a low heat. Carefully add the potatoes, turning them in the hot oil and seasoning them well. Return them to the oven and cook for about 20 minutes, then turn them over and cook for a further 20 minutes, until crisp and golden.

# Potato Gratin

The combinations of vegetables you can use for gratins are endless. The basic recipe here can be adapted for other root vegetables – see the Variations below for some of our favourites.

350ml **double cream**

150ml **milk**

3 cloves of **garlic**, crushed

**salt** and **freshly ground black pepper**

1kg **potatoes**, peeled and very thinly sliced (by hand or using a mandolin)

1 tablespoon grated **Gruyère cheese**

1 tablespoon grated **vegetarian Parmesan-style cheese**

1. Put the cream and milk into a large pan with the crushed garlic and bring to the boil. Remove from the heat, season well and allow to stand for 10 minutes.

2. Meanwhile, heat the oven to 170°C/325°F/ gas mark 3.

3. Tip the sliced potatoes into the pan and mix very well so that they are all coated with the cream mixture. Season again. Transfer to a gratin dish, arranging the slices in layers with a good distribution of cream (this can be done roughly or precisely).

4. Cover the dish with kitchen foil and bake in the oven for about 40 minutes, or until the potatoes are tender.

5. Remove the foil, sprinkle with the two cheeses and return the dish to the oven for a further 10 minutes, or until golden brown on top. Serve.

**VARIATIONS**

❀ Use 50:50 celeriac and potato.

❀ Mix thinly sliced fennel with the sliced potato and a tablespoon of finely chopped fresh rosemary.

❀ Mix sliced Jerusalem artichokes with the potatoes – but reduce the amount of liquid, as artichokes tend to be more watery. Cooked leeks can also be added.

❀ Make a porcini cream: reduce soaked and chopped dried porcini in their soaking liquid with fresh thyme leaves, then add cream and garlic. Use the porcini cream to make a gratin of potatoes or Jerusalem artichokes, or both.

❀ Adding chopped fresh chilli and rosemary to your garlic cream makes it a great base for a sweet potato and potato gratin.

❀ Cook thinly sliced beetroot with garlic, fresh thyme leaves and a little cream. Only a little cream is needed, as lots of liquid comes out of the beetroot.

❀ Add a handful of chopped wild garlic leaves and some chopped wet garlic to the cream before cooking the potatoes.

❀ For a dairy-free gratin, infuse a pinch of saffron threads in hot vegetable stock and use instead of cream to bake the potatoes with softened onions and a few bay leaves.

# Potato Salad

SERVES 4 • PREPARATION TIME: 10 MINUTES • COOKING TIME: 15 MINUTES • WF GF V

This is a mile away from the bland and often anaemic-looking potato salads that have given this classic dish a bad reputation.

750g **new** or **waxy potatoes**

1 tablespoon good **white wine vinegar**

1 tablespoon **olive oil**

**salt** and **freshly ground black pepper**

1 tablespoon **gherkins**, chopped

1 tablespoon **capers**, soaked in cold water and drained

1 tablespoon good-quality **mayonnaise**

1 tablespoon **crème fraîche**

2 teaspoons **Dijon mustard**

3 **hard-boiled eggs**, peeled and chopped

2 tablespoons **chopped mixed fresh herbs** (**chives**, **tarragon** and **dill**)

1. Bring a large pan of salted water to the boil, then add the potatoes and cook for 10–15 minutes, until tender. Drain, cut into small pieces and put into a bowl. While still warm, sprinkle with the vinegar and oil, then season well and allow to cool.

2. Mix the rest of the ingredients (except the eggs and herbs) in a bowl. Add the potatoes and fold in gently. Finally, sprinkle over the chopped eggs and herbs to garnish.

**VARIATIONS**

✿ Cook diced red onions in cider vinegar and a little brown sugar until the liquid is almost reduced. When the new potatoes are cooked, drain and toss in the red onion mixture with lots of olive oil and some blanched broad beans.

✿ Add sliced raw sugar snap peas to the hot cooked new potatoes with the olive oil and vinegar. Cover and allow to steam for 5 minutes. Scatter over lots of chopped fresh mint to serve.

✿ Toss sliced cooked new potatoes in olive oil and grill on each side on a heated griddle until just charred. Make a mustard caper dressing with 1 tablespoon soaked capers, roughly chopped, mixed with 2 tablespoons olive oil, 2 teaspoons grain mustard, 2 teaspoons honey, 1 tablespoon balsamic vinegar and 2 teaspoons chopped fresh mint. Arrange the grilled potatoes on a serving plate and drizzle over the dressing to serve.

✿ Chop peeled red peppers (or smoky piquillo peppers from a jar), toss with cooked new potatoes and drizzle with Tahini Dressing (see page 81).

✿ Mix cooked sweetcorn kernels with cooked new potatoes and dress with chopped fresh chilli, fresh coriander, lime juice and olive oil.

# Courgette Ceviche

SERVES 4 • PREPARATION TIME: 5 MINUTES • COOKING TIME: NONE • ♥ ✓ WF GF DF V

This dish works best when made with very fresh and small courgettes.

3 **courgettes**

½ teaspoon **salt**

grated zest and juice of 1 **lemon**

2 tablespoons **olive oil**

1. Slice the courgettes into thin strips, using a speed peeler. Put them into a colander, sprinkle with the salt and set aside for an hour.

2. Mix the lemon zest, juice and oil together in a bowl. Add the courgette strips and toss to coat, then serve immediately.

**TIPS**

* Try crumbling over some ricotta cheese and sprinkling toasted flaked almonds on top to serve.

# Stir-fried Fennel with Olives & Basil

SERVES 4 • PREPARATION TIME: 5 MINUTES • COOKING TIME: 1 MINUTE • ♥ ✓ WF GF DF V

Cooking the fennel briefly like this retains its crunch and fresh flavour.

2 heads of **fennel**

2 tablespoons **olive oil**

1 clove of **garlic**, crushed

1 teaspoon **fennel seeds**, ground

50g **black olives**, stoned and roughly chopped

50g **ready-cooked red peppers** (from a jar), peeled and chopped

juice of ½ an **orange**

a small bunch of **fresh basil**, shredded

**salt** and **freshly ground black pepper**

1. Trim the fennel and finely slice it, either by hand or using a mandolin.

2. Heat the oil in a large shallow frying pan. Add the sliced fennel, garlic and fennel seeds. Stir quickly for 1 minute, then remove from the heat.

3. Mix in the rest of the ingredients and season well.

**TIPS**

* Piquillo peppers make a lovely and slightly smoky addition to this dish.

* Try making this without cooking the fennel, leaving it raw and omitting the fennel seeds. Use the olive oil as the dressing, with a little balsamic vinegar.

# Celeriac Rémoulade

Below are two recipes for this classic dish … the Creole version from Jane and a light yoghurty version from Henry.

## Jane's Creole Rémoulade

SERVES 6 • PREPARATION TIME: 15 MINUTES
COOKING TIME: NONE • ♥ ✓ WF GF DF V

750g **celeriac**, peeled and grated

**salt** and **freshly ground black pepper**

1 bunch of **spring onions**, white and light green parts chopped

1 tablespoon chopped **fresh flat-leaf parsley**

1 clove of **garlic**, crushed

2 sticks of **celery**, chopped

1 tablespoon **coarse-grain mustard**

2 tablespoons **cider** or **tarragon vinegar**

1 teaspoon **ground paprika**

1 tablespoon grated **horseradish** (or 2 teaspoons **horseradish relish**)

100ml **olive oil**

2 tablespoons **capers**, soaked in cold water for 10 minutes, then drained

1.  Place the celeriac in a bowl and season.

2.  Put the spring onions, parsley, garlic, celery, mustard, vinegar, paprika and horseradish into a food processor and blend together, making sure they are well combined.

3.  With the machine still running, slowly add the olive oil until an emulsion is formed. Season and stir in the capers. Mix this dressing with the grated celeriac, check the seasoning and serve.

**TIPS**

* This can be garnished with grated hard-boiled eggs.

## Henry's Rémoulade

SERVES 4 • PREPARATION TIME: 10 MINUTES
COOKING TIME: 1 MINUTE • ♥ ✓ WF GF V

500g **celeriac**, peeled and grated

150ml thick **Greek yoghurt**

2 teaspoons **Dijon mustard**

juice of ½ a **lemon**

1 tablespoon chopped **fresh dill**

1 tablespoon chopped **gherkins**

**salt** and **freshly ground black pepper**

1.  Bring a large pan of salted water to the boil, then add the celeriac and blanch for 1 minute. Drain, refresh under running cold water and squeeze out excess moisture.

2.  Put the rest of the ingredients into a bowl and mix together. Stir in the grated celeriac, season well and serve.

JANE'S CREOLE REMOULADE

# French Beans & Tomatoes with Niçoise Dressing

SERVES 4 • PREPARATION TIME: 15 MINUTES • COOKING TIME: 3 MINUTES • ♥ ✓ WF GF DF V

300g **French beans**

200g **very ripe tomatoes**

1 tablespoon **capers**, soaked in lots of water

1 clove of **garlic**, crushed

1 tablespoon **red wine vinegar**

2 tablespoons **olive oil**

a small bunch of **fresh basil**

1 tablespoon **mixed olives**, chopped

3 **tomatoes**, chopped

**salt** and **freshly ground black pepper**

1. Top and tail the beans.

2. Slice the tomatoes in half and extract all the juice by forcing it through a sieve into a bowl. Add the capers, garlic, vinegar, oil and basil leaves. Blend with an immersion blender or in a blender.

3. Bring a pan of salted water to the boil, then add the beans and cook for about 3 minutes, until tender (just past the squeaky stage). Drain well.

4. While the beans are still hot, toss them in a bowl with the tomato dressing, chopped olives and tomatoes. Season well.

**TIPS**

* If you can find them, use salted capers as they have a better flavour, but they will need soaking and rinsing before using.

* This makes a good meal with a poached egg on top.

* Toast some chunks of stale ciabatta in a medium-hot oven to make croûtons and toss in the tomato dressing above. Yum.

* Use grilled courgettes or grilled aubergines in place of the French beans.

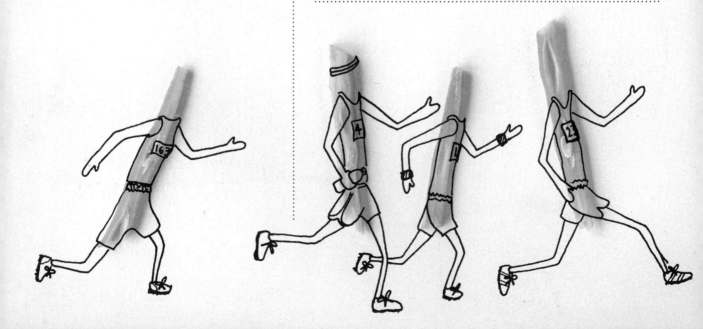

# Ben's Aubergine & Celery Caponata

SERVES 6 • PREPARATION TIME: 10 MINUTES • COOKING TIME: 25 MINUTES • ♥ WF GF DF V

This is a classic aubergine dish that has many variations. As with any caponata, cooking the vegetables separately is the key. It is important to get right the balance between the sugar, the vinegar and the salty ingredients.

2 **celery hearts** (the most tender centre parts)

3 tablespoons **olive oil**

2 large **aubergines**, cubed

2 **onions**, diced

1 clove of **garlic**, sliced

1 x 400g tin of good **tomatoes**, chopped and drained

**salt** and **freshly ground black pepper**, to taste

1 tablespoon **caster sugar**

50ml **red wine vinegar**

30g **pine nuts**, toasted

25g **salted capers**, rinsed well

200g pitted **green olives**

small bunch of **fresh basil**

1. Coarsely chop the celery, and blanch in boiling water for 1 minute. Drain and refresh under cold water.

2. Heat the olive oil in a large shallow frying pan and fry the aubergine cubes over a medium heat until brown. Remove from the pan with a slotted spoon and set aside.

3. In the same pan, fry the onions until softened. Add the celery, garlic and tomatoes and cook until the celery is soft and the tomatoes have reduced. Add a little salt and pepper, remembering that the olives and capers will add an extra hit of salt.

4. Add the aubergines, sugar, vinegar, pine nuts, capers and olives. Tear in the basil leaves and cook for 8–10 minutes. It is important for each vegetable to keep its own integrity and texture – the caponata should by no means be a mush – so make sure you use a large enough pan. Serve at room temperature.

BEN IN HIS MUM'S GARDEN, TAUNTON, 1984

Ben Bulger (see page 31) worked with me for a few years at the Field Kitchen in Devon. He is a brilliant chef and has now gone on to run the kitchens at The Magdalen Chapter hotel in Exeter. This is one of the dishes that he often cooked as part of an antipasti selection in the evening. Ben trained in some of the best kitchens in the country and is technically excellent, but still prefers to cook real unpretentious food that is accessible to all.

JANE

# Thai Cucumber Salad

SERVES 4 • PREPARATION TIME: 10 MINUTES • COOKING TIME: NONE • ♥ WF GF DF V

This is a very fresh side dish that makes a cooling addition to a spicy main.

2 medium **cucumbers**

**salt**

¼ teaspoon **chilli flakes**

1 tablespoon **soft brown sugar**

2 tablespoons **rice vinegar**

1 tablespoon very finely chopped **red onion**

1 tablespoon very finely chopped **spring onions**

1. Using a speed peeler, peel away lengthways strips of skin from the cucumbers while still leaving some green ridges.

2. Slice as thinly as possible and put into a colander. Salt generously, then set aside over a bowl for at least 40 minutes to extract excess liquid.

3. Mix together the rest of the ingredients in a bowl to make a dressing.

4. Using a clean tea towel, squeeze out as much moisture as possible from the cucumbers. Put into a serving bowl and stir in the dressing.

5. Chill until ready to serve.

**TIPS**

* To ring the changes, top with toasted chopped peanuts, fresh chilli and chopped fresh mint.

* Sesame oil and sesame seeds can also be added to build more flavour.

* If you like more heat, increase the amount of chilli or swap the dried chilli flakes for chopped fresh chillies.

# Malaysian Tomato Salad

SERVES 4 • PREPARATION TIME: 10 MINUTES • COOKING TIME: 2 MINUTES • ♥ WF GF DF V

This is a refreshing change from the usual tomato salad with basil.

2 tablespoons **desiccated coconut**

1½ tablespoons **kecap manis** (sweet soy sauce)

2 teaspoons **dark brown sugar**

2 teaspoons **rice vinegar**

2 **red chillies**, deseeded and finely sliced

8 large ripe **tomatoes**, or 4 **beef tomatoes**

4 **spring onions**, finely sliced

1. Dry-fry the coconut in a non-stick pan, tossing occasionally, over a medium heat until golden. Set aside.

2. Put the kecap manis, sugar, vinegar, chillies and 2 teaspoons of the toasted coconut into a bowl and stir to make a dressing.

3. Slice the tomatoes thinly and arrange in a serving dish.

4. Drizzle with the dressing and sprinkle with the rest of the roasted coconut and the spring onions before serving.

**T I P S**

* The dressing in this recipe would be a great accompaniment to fried aubergines, fried tofu or blanched spinach.

# Fried Courgettes

SERVES 4 • PREPARATION TIME: 15 MINUTES • COOKING TIME: 10 MINUTES • ♥ ✓ WF GF DF V

In southern Italy the courgettes for this dish are dried outside in the sun before frying, which makes them very crisp as a result. In the UK that could be a problem and oven-drying does not create the same effect, so this method, from Jane's time at The River Café, relies on very thinly sliced courgettes.

750g **courgettes**

**sunflower oil**, for deep-frying

1 tablespoon good-quality **red wine vinegar**

2 cloves of **garlic**, sliced and cut into very fine spikes

2 **red chillies**, deseeded and cut across into fine strips

a small bunch of **fresh mint**, leaves picked and cut across into fine strips

**salt** and **freshly ground black pepper**

1. Cut the courgettes across into very thin rounds, using a mandolin.

2. Put the courgette slices into a bowl of iced water and leave to soak for about 40 minutes, then drain and dry well on tea towels.

3. Heat the sunflower oil to 190°C in a large heavy-based pan and cook the courgettes in small batches, removing each batch when lightly browned and draining them on kitchen paper.

4. Spread the cooked courgettes on a large serving plate and sprinkle with the vinegar. Scatter over the garlic, chillies and mint, and season well.

**TIPS**

\* This method can also be used for aubergines – remember to salt the aubergine slices first to remove any excess moisture.

LEON, 1965

# Katarina's Cheesy Balls

MAKES ABOUT 20 BALLS • PREPARATION TIME:10 MINUTES • COOKING TIME: 5 MINUTES • V Ⓥ

This makes a great nibble to serve at a drinks party or as part of an antipasti selection.

**2 egg whites**

320g **Gruyère cheese**, grated

large pinch of **cayenne pepper**

**sunflower oil**, for deep-frying

100g **dried breadcrumbs**
(Japanese panko crumbs
are best)

1. In a large bowl, whisk the egg whites using an electric hand whisk until almost holding peaks.

2. Fold in the grated Gruyère and add the cayenne. Form the mixture into small walnut-sized balls.

3. Heat the oil to 180°C in a deep-fryer or heavy-based pan. Roll the balls in the breadcrumbs and deep-fry in batches for a few minutes until golden brown. Drain on kitchen paper and serve.

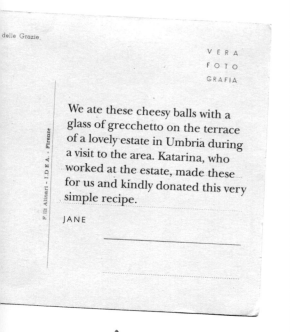

delle Grazie

VERA FOTO GRAFIA

P.lli Alinari · I.D.E.A. · Firenze

We ate these cheesy balls with a glass of grecchetto on the terrace of a lovely estate in Umbria during a visit to the area. Katarina, who worked at the estate, made these for us and kindly donated this very simple recipe.

JANE

## TIPS

* Deep-fried sage leaves make a great garnish sprinkled over the balls.

* Try stuffing a small cube of mozzarella into the centre of each ball.

* Other cheeses can be used if you prefer.

# Franco's Panzarotti

FAMILY & FRIENDS RECIPE

MAKES ABOUT 50 PANZAROTTI • PREPARATION TIME: 20 MINUTES • COOKING TIME: 10 MINUTES • V Ⓥ

Panzarotti are normally made with fresh pasta squares, but here we've used wonton wrappers, which are available from most Chinese supermarkets. They make a quick, impressive party snack.

200g **ricotta cheese**

200g **mozzarella cheese**

60g **vegetarian Parmesan-style cheese**, grated

grated **nutmeg**

1 tablespoon chopped **fresh flat-leaf parsley**

**salt** and **freshly ground black pepper**

1 packet of **wonton wrappers**

**sunflower oil**, for deep-frying

1. Roughly chop the ricotta and mozzarella and put into a bowl with the Parmesan. Add the nutmeg and parsley and season very well.

2. Lay out the wonton wrappers on a clean, dry tea towel, a few at a time. Place a good teaspoon of the cheese mix in the centre of each one, then dampen the edges of each wonton with a little water, using a pastry brush, and fold over one point to meet the other to make a triangular parcel. Seal the edges with your fingers.

3. Heat the oil to 180°C in a deep-fryer or heavy-based pan and deep-fry the wontons, a few at a time, until golden and crisp. Drain on kitchen paper and serve.

This recipe comes from Franco Taruschio, the legendary chef who ran The Walnut Tree near Abergavenny for many years. It was his idea to use wonton wrappers instead of pasta, and they really do work well as a substitute.

JANE

**TIPS**

* Try using a different herbs such as chopped chives, basil, tarragon and chervil.

* You could add a little chopped cooked spinach to the cheese mixture.

* We have drizzled a little truffle oil into the cheese mix to great effect.

* These are good served with a little grated Parmesan-style cheese or pecorino … or, for an extra indulgence, a drizzle of truffle honey.

FRANCO, AGE 8, MONTEFANO, ITALY

# Lentils with Peas, Broad Beans & Mint

SERVES 6 (AS A SIDE) • PREPARATION TIME: 5 MINUTES • COOKING TIME: 40 MINUTES • ♥ ✓ WF* GF* DF V
*UNLESS SERVED ON BRUSCHETTA

This is great as a side, but equally good to eat on its own on grilled bruschetta.

100g **green lentils**
(or **Puy lentils**)

1 tablespoon **olive oil**, plus
extra for drizzling

**salt** and **freshly ground
black pepper**

1 **onion**, finely chopped

3 cloves of **garlic**, crushed

150g shelled **broad beans**

150g shelled **peas**

150g **sugar snap peas**,
trimmed and sliced

1 tablespoon chopped
**fresh mint**

1. Put the lentils into a pan and add cold water to cover them by about 1cm. Bring to the boil, then reduce the heat and simmer for about 20 minutes, or until tender. Drain, then drizzle with olive oil, season well and set aside.

2. Heat 1 tablespoon of oil in a medium pan, then add the onion and cook over a medium heat for 5 minutes. Add the garlic, stir well and cook for another 2 minutes.

3. Bring a pan of salted water to the boil and cook the broad beans for 2–3 minutes, or until tender. Drain well and add immediately to the onion mixture.

4. Now stir in the lentils, peas and sugar snap peas and cook together over a low heat for 5 minutes.

5. To finish the dish, season well, add lots of chopped mint and drizzle with good olive oil.

**TIPS**

* If your broad beans are large it may be necessary to remove their rubbery outer skins after blanching.

* Cooked artichoke wedges can be added with the peas to make this into a more substantial dish.

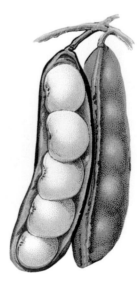

# Coleslaw

There are so many different versions of the humble coleslaw that a whole chapter could be dedicated to them. At Leon we have been playing with different mixes since the day we first opened. Here, we have given a simple recipe for a very basic slaw and followed it with three variations. If you want to experiment with your own, keep an eye on acidity (we like it sharp), seasoning, different textures and colour. Basically, however, the rules are as follows: if it tastes good raw and you can shred it, chuck it in.

½ a **white cabbage**, finely shredded

300g **carrots**, peeled and grated

½ a **red onion**, very finely sliced

1 clove of **garlic**, crushed

1 tablespoon **crème fraîche**

1 tablespoon **thick natural yoghurt**

1 teaspoon **Dijon mustard**

**salt** and **freshly ground black pepper**

1. Put all the ingredients into a large bowl and mix together. Season well.

**VARIATIONS**

✿ **Middle Eastern slaw**: mix together grated red cabbage, carrot, celeriac and squash. Dress with balsamic vinegar, olive oil and orange juice (and grated zest). Stir in toasted pine nuts, pomegranate seeds and shredded mint, and season well.

✿ **Waldorf slaw**: shredded white cabbage and fennel mixed with chopped celery and apple. Dress with pure mayonnaise or a mixture of mayonnaise, yoghurt and crème fraîche. Fold in thinly sliced onions, toasted walnuts, golden raisins, chives and dill, and season well.

✿ **Asian slaw**: mix together shredded cabbage, thinly sliced red pepper, grated carrot, finely chopped French beans and diced tomato. Make a dressing of lime juice, palm sugar (or soft brown sugar), chopped red chilli, crushed garlic, fresh coriander and crushed peanuts.

**COLESLAW PHOTO KEY**

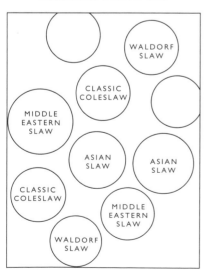

WALDORF SLAW

CLASSIC COLESLAW

MIDDLE EASTERN SLAW

ASIAN SLAW

ASIAN SLAW

CLASSIC COLESLAW

MIDDLE EASTERN SLAW

WALDORF SLAW

# Vegetable Purée with Mushrooms

FAMILY
& FRIENDS
RECIPE

SERVES 6 • PREPARATION TIME: 15 MINUTES • COOKING TIME: 30 MINUTES • ♥ ✓ WF GF V

This is one of Henry's mum Jossy's recipes. Nobody ever quite guesses the ingredients of this deliciously light, smooth purée. It can be served on individual plates as a mushroom first course or on one round plate as part of a main course; it is eaten cold, so can be prepared ahead.

1 large **aubergine**

½ a large **cauliflower**

1 medium **red pepper**

4–5 large cloves of **garlic**

a 4–5cm piece of **fresh ginger**

¼–½ a **nutmeg**

juice of ½ a small **lemon**

2 tablespoons **whole natural yoghurt**

**sea salt** and **freshly ground black pepper**

**sunflower oil**

250–300g **chestnut mushrooms**, thinly sliced

120–140g **shiitake mushrooms**, thinly sliced

2 rounded teaspoons **cumin seeds**

a large handful of **fresh coriander leaves**, roughly chopped

**extra virgin olive oil**

1. Heat the grill to its highest and place a large piece of kitchen foil in the grill pan. Pierce a slit in the aubergine and put it on top of the foil. Leave under the grill, turning once or twice, until the skin is completely black and cracked all over.

2. While this is happening you can prepare the other ingredients. Cut the cauliflower into florets, but leave on most of the stalk part. Cut the red pepper in half, discard the stem and seeds, and chop into very small pieces. Peel the garlic and ginger and chop finely.

3. When the aubergine is all black, remove it from the grill, enclose it in the foil and leave to cool. When cool enough to handle, scrape all the mushy insides out and put it into a food processor, discarding the burnt skin.

4. Steam the cauliflower pieces until really soft and add to the food processor. Grate the nutmeg finely, add to the mixture and blitz. Then add the lemon juice and yoghurt and blitz very thoroughly again until you have a smooth purée. Season to taste with salt and pepper, then transfer the purée into a bowl, cool and chill in the fridge.

5. Put 4 tablespoons of sunflower oil into a large deep frying pan over a medium heat. Add the mushrooms and red pepper and stir over the heat until both are really soft. Add the chopped garlic and ginger and the cumin seeds and continue stirring over the heat for another 4–5 minutes – don't let the garlic burn. Finally, season with a little sea salt and black pepper, leave until cold, then stir in the chopped coriander.

6. Spoon the chilled purée on to individual plates or one round serving plate, spreading it out. Pile the mushroom mixture in the centre. Just before serving, drizzle olive oil round the edges.

JOSSY, DARTMOOR, 1978

## OUR FAVOURITE PURÉES

❀ Cook peeled chopped parsnips in milk until tender. Drain and place in a food processor with crushed garlic, lemon juice and a handful of ground almonds. Blitz with a little olive oil, season and serve with toasted almonds.

❀ Brown fennel wedges in a little olive oil over a high heat, then reduce the heat and cook slowly with garlic and a little chopped rosemary. When soft, add lemon juice, season and purée in a blender.

❀ Cook loads of sliced onions very slowly with some grated lemon zest in olive oil and butter for about an hour, without colouring. Remove the zest before blending with a little lemon juice.

❀ Cook onions slowly in olive oil with cauliflower florets until the cauli is tender. Blitz with a little milk, Parmesan-style cheese and truffle oil.

❀ Creamed Kale (see page 234).

❀ Creamed corn: cook sweetcorn kernels in butter, with onion, red chillies, thyme, and a pinch of cumin, for 20 minutes, until caramelized. Deglaze with a little white wine and cover with vegetable stock. Simmer until tender. Season well and pass through the coarse blade of a food mill, or pulse in a blender or food processor.

# PICKLES
# & CHUTNEYS

LEON

# Bruno's Piccalilli

SERVES 6 • PREPARATION TIME: 15 MINUTES • COOKING TIME: 15 MINUTES • ♥ ✓ WF GF DF V

Piccalilli is one of life's great pickles. Here is a Frenchman's take on it – Henry's first boss, chef Bruno Loubet. It is a fresh version, so keep it in the fridge. Bruno used to serve this with grilled mackerel.

4 tablespoons **olive oil**

150g **carrots**, diced

1 **red pepper**, diced

150g **fennel**, diced

150g **celery**, diced

150g **onion**, diced

200g **cauliflower**, broken into small florets

2 cloves of **garlic**, crushed

1 **bay leaf**

1 teaspoon grated **fresh ginger**

1 teaspoon **turmeric**

½ teaspoon **curry powder**

100ml **white wine**

1 tablespoon **coarse-grain mustard**

**salt** and **freshly ground black pepper**

100g **courgettes**, diced

½ tablespoon **fresh coriander**

1. Heat the oil in a large pan and add the carrots, red pepper, fennel, celery, onion and cauliflower. Cook for 3 minutes over a medium heat, stirring well to stop the vegetables sticking.

2. Add the rest of the ingredients apart from the courgettes and coriander. Bring to the boil, then reduce the heat to medium and simmer for 5 minutes. Add the courgettes and continue to cook for a further 3 minutes. Remove from the heat, season and stir in the coriander.

3. Leave to cool, then chill. Keep in a bowl in the fridge for up to a week.

BRUNO (MIDDLE), ILE D'OLERON, 1969

# Spiced Pumpkin Jam

MAKES 300ML • PREPARATION TIME: 10 MINUTES • COOKING TIME: 45 MINUTES • WF GF DG V

This jam is sweet and slightly spicy. Spread it on hot buttered toast or crumpets.

500g **pumpkin flesh**, diced

a 2cm piece of **fresh ginger**, grated

1 **red chilli**, chopped

½ teaspoon **ground turmeric**

1 teaspoon **ground cinnamon**

seeds from 3 **cardamom pods**, crushed

125ml **cider vinegar**

125ml **water**

200g **soft brown sugar**

1. Place all the ingredients except the sugar in a heavy-based pan and bring to a simmer. Continue to cook over a low heat for about 30 minutes, or until the pumpkin flesh is soft.

2. Add the sugar and turn up the heat to medium. Cook for approximately 15 minutes, stirring, until the mixture starts to thicken. The pumpkin should have broken down to a smooth paste.

3. Transfer to sterilized jars (see Tips) and keep in the fridge for up to 2 weeks.

**TIPS**

* Squash may be used instead of pumpkin, but cooking times may differ.

* To sterilize jars for chutney, put clean, washed and dried jam jars or bottles into a cold oven with the lids off. Turn the oven on to 160°C/325°F/gas mark 3 and put the timer on for 20 minutes. When the timer goes, turn off the oven, leaving the jars inside to cool slightly. Pour in your chutney while the jars are still hot.

BY AIRMAIL
PAR AVION

DAVID, AGE 5,
RIVER DART PARK, DEVON

My son, David, and I spent one Christmas glamping in a national park in Sri Lanka, on a birdwatching trip. We were lucky enough to share our meals with a lovely Sri Lankan/ Swiss family and they told me about this dish that they cooked at home when pumpkins were in season.

JANE

# Runner Bean Chutney

MAKES 1.5 LITRES • PREPARATION TIME: 15 MINUTES • COOKING TIME: 35 MINUTES • ♥ WF GF DF V

A very Devon chutney to make when there is a glut of runner beans. This recipe was given to us by the ladies at the country market in Kingsbridge, which is held in the foyer of the Reel Cinema every Wednesday morning.

900g **runner beans** (weight after stringing), sliced

4 **onions**, chopped

680g **demerara sugar**

850ml **malt vinegar**

1½ tablespoons **ground turmeric**

1½ tablespoons **English mustard powder**

1½ tablespoons **cornflour**

1. Bring a large pan of salted water to the boil. Add the runner beans and onions, boil for 2 minutes, then drain and return the vegetables to the pan.

2. Add the sugar and 700ml of the vinegar, bring to the boil, then reduce the heat and simmer for 15 minutes.

3. Put the turmeric, mustard and cornflour into a small bowl and stir in the remaining vinegar. Add this mixture to the beans and simmer for a further 15 minutes.

4. Allow to cool, then put into sterilized jars (see Tips on page 267). Keeps for up to 6 months before opening.

# Lyn's Marrow Chutney

FAMILY & FRIENDS RECIPE

MAKES APPROX. 2 LITRES • PREPARATION TIME: 10 MINUTES (PLUS SALTING OVERNIGHT)
COOKING TIME: 50 MINUTES • ♥ WF GF DF V

For the dreaded marrow glut. Large courgettes can be used instead of marrows.

1.8kg **marrows**
900g **onions**
2 teaspoons **salt**
1.1 litres **cider vinegar**
4 teaspoons **ground turmeric**
60g **mustard powder**
900g **sugar**
1 sachet of **pickling spice**

1. Peel and deseed the marrows, then slice thinly. Chop the onions finely. Put the marrow and onions into a bowl, then sprinkle with the salt and rub it through the vegetables with your fingers. Leave in a colander overnight (place the colander on top of a bowl or tray to catch the excess liquid).

2. Next day, tip the marrow and onions into a large pan and add 1 litre of the vinegar. Bring to the boil, then reduce the heat and simmer for about 30 minutes, or until the marrow is soft and 'pulpy'.

3. Make a paste by mixing the remaining 100ml of vinegar in a bowl with the turmeric and mustard powder. Set aside.

4. Add the sugar to the pan and stir until dissolved. Now stir in the reserved turmeric paste and add the pickling spice.

5. Bring back to the boil and cook for another 15–20 minutes, or until the chutney has thickened. Decant into sterilized jars (see Tips on page 267).

Kate has worked with me for several years and also helped on some of the photo shoots for this book. She is pictured with her daughter Miriam on page 58. This recipe has been donated by her mum's long-time friend Lyn. Kate recommended this recipe to me, as it is one that she frequently finds herself eating directly from the jar. Like the Runner Bean Chutney (see page 268) this is a local Devon recipe, and has been passed around friends before landing here in this book.

JANE

LYN, DEVON, 1953

# Jonnie's Sauerkraut

MAKES 1.5 LITRES • PREPARATION TIME: 15 MINUTES • COOKING TIME: NONE • ♥ ✓ WF GF DF V

Alsatian pickled cabbage, to eat fresh with lunch or to cook with wine, potatoes (and … er … smoked meats).

1kg **white cabbage**, finely sliced

20g **sea salt**

¼ teaspoon **caraway seeds**

7 **juniper berries**

1. Put the cabbage into a large bowl. Add the salt and massage it into the cabbage so that the salt is evenly distributed and moisture begins to form. Mix in the caraway seeds and juniper berries.

2. Pack the cabbage into a clean 1.5 litre kilner jar (or similar), shoving it in with the end of a rolling pin to make sure it is compact.

3. Place a washed cabbage leaf on top, followed by a small weight (for example, a scrubbed and boiled stone or a small glass tumbler filled with water). This will help to keep the cabbage under the liquid.

4. Pour over enough water to cover the cabbage leaf and the weight. This is important, as any exposed cabbage may go off and ruin the batch. Leave somewhere cool and out of direct sunlight.

5. Once a week, open the jar to let out any gas that has formed. If you notice any white bloom on top, DO NOT worry: this is perfectly normal and can be scooped out – the kraut underneath will be fine.

6. Check after about 4 weeks to see how sour it is and then leave for another 2 weeks to mature nicely. It is now ready to eat. Store in the fridge for up to 3 months, but make sure the kraut is under the liquid. Once open, consume within 2 weeks.

I got into a kraut-making phase quite by accident. I had a massive glut of cabbage leftover from our veg box, and one night I shredded the lot for sauerkraut. It's remarkably easy and, if you like cooking experiments, really satisfying. You don't need to wait all that long to eat it. You can try it every few days and enjoy it as it gets tangier. At one point I had a huge vat that I used to keep on the go, filling it underneath with fresh cabbage and eating it from the top.

HENRY

JONNIE, NORTH DEVON, 1978

JONNIE, SARAH AND LEELA ROSE GUEST, COOMBE FARM STUDIOS, DITTISHAM, 2013

## A FEW WORDS FROM JONNIE ON THE BENEFITS OF FERMENTED VEG

Traditional cultures have been fermenting foods for thousands of years, not just to make alcohol, but also to prolong the life of vegetables, fruit and meat through the winter months. Sauerkraut is simple to make, but scientifically satisfying. By shredding the cabbage finely and adding salt we start an alchemical process that results ultimately in the formation of *Lactobacillus plantarum*, which creates a nutrient-rich, sour-tasting, crunchy cabbage that will keep for many months in the right conditions.

The explorer Captain James Cook, wanting to halt the demise of his crew from scurvy (a disease caused by lack of vitamin C), started to take barrels of sauerkraut on his voyages and the health of his crew improved dramatically. Sauerkraut is also abundant in vitamin B1 (retinol), which is beneficial for good eyesight and the immune system, B2 (riboflavin), which helps the production of red blood cells, needed to carry oxygen around the body, and B3 (niacin), which helps to lower cholesterol. The *Lactobacillus* which gives it its sour taste is also helpful to our intestinal flora, which aids our digestive capabilities. Some people buy it in tablet form, which is not as enjoyable as eating fresh-tasting homemade unpasteurized sauerkraut. I make it because I enjoy the process and I eat it because I love it!

# Kimchee

MAKES 2 LITRES • PREPARATION TIME: 15 MINUTES (PLUS SOAKING OVERNIGHT)
COOKING TIME: NONE • ♥ ✓ WF GF DF V

Korea's national dish is made from fermented vegetables and chilli. It is nutritious and is traditionally used as a base for braises and stews, but it is also often served on the table as a condiment. It makes a good cleansing dinner with steamed or boiled rice.

1kg **Chinese cabbage**

1 **daikon** (or 200g **red radishes**)

120g **salt**

250ml **water**

2 x 4cm pieces of **fresh ginger**, minced

8 cloves of **garlic**, crushed

1 tablespoon **soy sauce**

1 bunch of **spring onions**, chopped

3 tablespoons **Korean chilli powder**

1 **apple**, cored and cut into small dice

1. Cut the Chinese cabbage into 4cm slices. Peel the daikon and slice thinly on a mandolin. Put the cabbage and daikon into a large bowl.

2. Dissolve the salt in the water and pour over the cabbage and daikon. Mix well, then cover the bowl and leave to soak overnight.

3. Next day, drain the veg, squeezing out as much moisture as possible. Place in a large bowl.

4. Put the ginger, garlic and soy sauce into a food processor and blend together to make a paste. Put the paste into a bowl and stir in the spring onions, chilli powder and diced apple. Add to the bowl of cabbage and daikon and toss until the leaves are well coated.

5. Pack into glass jars, pressing down well. If using screwtop jars, screw the lids on the jars (but not too tightly), then place them on a tray and leave at room temperature for 2–3 days.

6. After the 2–3 days, place in the fridge. The kimchee will be at its best after 2 weeks but it should be eaten within a month.

# Pickled Celery

SERVES 4–6 • PREPARATION TIME: 10 MINUTES • COOKING TIME: 20 MINUTES • WF GF DF V

This is a quick dish and is lovely served warm with ricotta or goat's cheese.

200g **sticks of celery**

100g **sugar**

juice of 1 **lemon**

150ml **water**

1. Wash the celery and cut it into very small cubes. Put it into a heavy-based saucepan and add the rest of the ingredients.

2. Bring to the boil, then continue to cook over a high heat, stirring constantly, until the celery caramelizes (about 20 minutes). Remove from the heat and serve warm.

PIETRO FORAGING FOR MUSHROOMS, AGE 6, MONTEGROSSO, ITALY

This recipe is from a restaurant in Puglia called Anticha Sapori. The chef, Pietro Zito, bases many of his dishes on foraged wild food and vegetables from his garden. The night before I visited his restaurant I had been due to demonstrate at a food festival. But when taking the stage in front of Puglia's culinary great and good, I tripped and fell Buster Keaton-style off the front of the stage on to the hard marble below. Pietro soothed my bruised body and ego the next day with a twenty-six-course lunch, held especially for us. It was staggering. JANE

# Pickled Turnips

MAKES 2 LITRES • PREPARATION TIME: 10 MINUTES • COOKING TIME: 5 MINUTES • WF GF DF V

This inexpensive Middle Eastern pickle is surprisingly moreish, and takes on the most beautiful deep pink colour from the beetroot. Their good on their own, as part of a mezze or in a sandwich.

70g **salt**

3 **bay leaves**

900ml **water**

300ml **white wine vinegar**

900g **turnips**

150g **beetroot**

100g **dried figs**

5 cloves of **garlic**

1. Put the salt into a pan with the bay leaves and 250ml of the water and place over a medium heat until the salt has dissolved. Remove from the heat and add the vinegar and the rest of the water. Stir well to combine.

2. Peel the turnips and beetroot and slice 5mm thick. Thinly slice the figs and the garlic.

3. In clean, dry jars layer up the turnips with the beetroot, figs and garlic. Pour over the vinegar solution, making sure the vegetables are covered by the liquid.

4. Leave at room temperature for a week, then refrigerate. The pickles should be eaten within 6 weeks.

**TIPS**

* Celery leaves can be added along with dried chillies, if you like a bit of a kick.

# PUDDINGS & CAKES

It is a bit of a cheat having a pudding chapter
in a book about vegetables, but Jane is the
universally acknowledged Queen of Puddings.
I didn't want you to miss out.

HENRY

LEON

# Rhubarb & Strawberry Crumble Sundae

SERVES 4 • PREPARATION TIME: 20 MINUTES • COOKING TIME: 20 MINUTES • V Ⓥ

So easy. So good. This is basically an assembly job, with just a little cooking at the beginning.

150ml **double cream**, whipped

4 scoops of **vanilla ice cream**

4 tablespoons **thick custard**

### FOR THE CRUMBLE

50g **plain flour**

30g **cold butter**, cut into small pieces

2 tablespoons **caster sugar**

50g **amaretti biscuits**, crushed

### FOR THE RHUBARB COMPOTE

150g **strawberries**, quartered

1 x **Rhubarb & Orange Compote** recipe (see page 40)

### FOR THE SAUCE

100g **strawberries**

1 tablespoon **caster sugar**

a drop of **vanilla extract**

juice of 1 **orange**

1. Heat the oven to 160°C/325°F/gas mark 3. To make the crumble topping, put the flour into a bowl and rub in the butter until the mixture resembles breadcrumbs. Stir in the sugar and crushed amaretti. Spread on a baking tray and bake in the oven for 20 minutes. Set aside to cool.

2. Stir the quartered strawberries into the rhubarb compote.

3. Blend all the sauce ingredients to a purée in a blender, then pass the purée through a sieve.

4. To assemble, divide half the compote between four sundae glasses and top with the cream. Next add the strawberry sauce and ice cream, followed by the rest of the compote and the custard.

5. Top with the crumble mix, then serve.

### VARIATIONS

✿ This sundae can be made with all sorts of fruit combinations. All you need is a fruit compote and/or sauce, custard, ice cream, or whipped cream and something for texture such as crumble or nuts. Serious adult versions could have booze in, too. Try the following combos:

- Banana with toffee and chocolate.
- Raspberry, peach and flaked almonds.
- Pear with caramelized pecans and butterscotch or chocolate sauce.

# Joyce's Sticky Toffee Puddings

SERVES 8–10 • PREPARATION TIME: 15 MINUTES, PLUS COOLING • COOKING TIME: 1 HOUR 30 MINUTES • V Ⓥ

This was the most requested pudding at the Field Kitchen. Soak your dried fruit early so that it has time to cool before you start cooking.

90g **dried apricots**

90g **dried dates**

300ml **boiling water**

1 teaspoon **bicarbonate of soda**

50g **butter**, softened, plus extra for greasing

150g **caster sugar**

1 **duck egg** or 2 small **hen eggs**

225g **self-raising flour**

1 teaspoon **baking powder**

### FOR THE TOPPING

220g **dark muscovado sugar**

120g **butter**

120ml **double cream**

JOYCE, BIRMINGHAM, 1938

1. Chop the dried fruit finely in a food processor. Place in a bowl and pour over the boiling water. Stir in the bicarb and set aside to cool.

2. Butter two 900ml (14cm) pudding bowls.

3. Place all the topping ingredients in a pan. Bring to a simmer, stirring until the butter has melted and you have a dark glossy sauce. Simmer for 2 minutes, then pour half the mixture into one bowl and the rest into the other.

4. Cream together the butter and sugar until light and fluffy. Add the egg(s) and mix well. Sift the flour with the baking powder and fold in. Stir in the cooled apricot mix.

5. Divide the cake mix between the two bowls. It may seem very wet, but do not fret! Cover each bowl with kitchen foil and secure with string.

6. These puddings now need to be steamed for 1½ hours. If you have access to a steamer, great, but the other way to do this is to place the bowls on a trivet at the bottom of a large pan and pour in boiling water to come halfway up the sides. Cover the pan and keep the water at a simmer, but remember to check that the water level doesn't get too low.

7. Lift the bowls out of the water and turn the puddings out on to a serving dish. Serve with cream or custard.

### TIPS

* This pudding can be made using either all dates or all apricots. We also used to put in a few prunes, figs and brandy at Christmas time.

FAMILY & FRIENDS RECIPE

Joyce Molyneux of The Carved Angel in Dartmouth generally served this pudding for a Sunday lunch, along with her acclaimed marmalade roll. There was such a sense of generosity on these occasions. The whole pudding was taken to the table so that the diners could choose as much or as little as they liked. We all developed major arm muscles when on front-of-house duty.

JANE

# Vicky's Sticky Rhubarb Pudding

SERVES 6–8 • PREPARATION TIME: 15 MINUTES • COOKING TIME: 50 MINUTES • V Ⓥ

Sticky. Toffy-ee. But with a lovely citrusy rhubarb tang. Pouring the boiling water over your pudding mix is disconcerting, but it works. Just make sure you use a deep enough ovenproof dish when you start the recipe.

100g **dark muscovado sugar**

175g **self-raising flour**

1 **egg**, beaten

125ml **milk**

50g **butter**, melted, plus extra for greasing

1 teaspoon **vanilla extract**

grated zest of 1 **orange**

500g **rhubarb**, trimmed and cut into 1cm pieces

**FOR THE TOPPING**

150g **dark muscovado sugar**

25g **butter**, cut into small pieces

juice of 1 **orange**

300ml **boiling water**

1. Heat the oven to 190°C/375°F/gas mark 5. Put the sugar and flour into a large bowl and mix together.

2. Beat the egg in a bowl with the milk and melted butter. Add the vanilla and orange zest. Pour the egg mixture into the flour and whisk to make a smooth batter.

3. Fold half the rhubarb into the batter and place the other half in a large buttered pudding bowl or deep ovenproof dish. Pour the batter over the top.

4. To make the topping, sprinkle the sugar and diced butter over the batter. Mix the orange juice with the boiling water and pour over the top of the pudding.

5. Bake in the oven for 45–55 minutes, or until browned on top and firm to the touch. Serve.

VICKY WITH TINKER THE CAT, PUDSEY, 1975

I discovered this pudding while on a fishing trip in the middle of the Indian Ocean. Fish were scarce that day, so I fell into conversation with a fellow fisherwoman Vicky Whiteley. She and her husband Bryn are farmers (and bee keepers) who sell their produce at a farm shop near Pudsey in Yorkshire in the middle of the Rhubarb Triangle. No sooner had I extracted her special rhubarb pudding recipe from her when I hooked the biggest fish of the day. Double win.

JANE

« L'ULTIMA CENA »
Leonardo da Vinci

Printed in Italy

Milano, Refettorio di S. Maria delle Grazi

# Parsnip, Cashew & Coconut Cake

MAKES I CAKE (ENOUGH FOR 8–10) • PREPARATION TIME: 15 MINUTES • COOKING TIME: 30 MINUTES • WF GF V

YOU MUST MAKE THIS CAKE! Unbelievably moist and delicious, it makes a great alternative to carrot cake and can be filled either with a sweetened lime cream (see Tips) or with white chocolate cream cheese icing, as here.

250g **butter**, softened, plus extra for greasing

250g **caster sugar**

4 **eggs**

150g **rice flour**

2 teaspoons **baking powder**

100g **desiccated coconut**

200g **cashew nuts**, finely chopped

250g **parsnips**, finely grated

approximately 4 tablespoons **milk**

**FOR THE WHITE CHOCOLATE CREAM CHEESE ICING**

100g **white chocolate**

200g **cream cheese**

75g **butter**, softened

few drops of **vanilla extract**

300g **icing sugar**, sifted

**TIPS**

* For an extra flourish, sprinkle toasted coconut and chopped cashew nuts on top to decorate.

* For a sweetened lime cream as an alternative filling, fold the seeds of a vanilla pod into whipped cream and add the grated zest and juice of a lime with a little sifted icing sugar.

1. Heat the oven to 150°C/300°F/gas mark 2. Grease two 22cm cake tins and line them with baking parchment.

2. Cream together the butter and sugar in a mixing bowl, then add the eggs one by one, beating after each addition.

3. In a second bowl, sift the rice flour with the baking powder and mix well. Add the coconut, cashews and grated parsnip.

4. Combine the two bowls of ingredients together, adding the milk slowly, until the cake mixture reaches 'dropping' consistency.

5. Divide the mixture between the two cake tins and bake in the oven for 30 minutes, or until a skewer comes out clean. Set aside to cool.

6. To make the icing, break up the white chocolate and melt it in a large heatproof bowl set over a pan of simmering water, making sure the bowl doesn't touch the surface of the water. Leave to cool a little.

7. Add the cream cheese, butter and vanilla to the melted chocolate and beat together. Gradually beat in the icing sugar.

8. Use half the icing to sandwich the two cakes together, then spread the rest of the icing over the top. Leave to set a little before serving.

# Pina Colada Pavlova

SERVES 6–8 • PREPARATION TIME: 15 MINUTES • COOKING TIME: 1 HOUR 30 MINUTES • WF GF V

This is a tried and tested basic pavlova method, but the real test is in 'knowing your oven' and finding the best temperature/cooking time to suit it.

### FOR THE PAVLOVA

180ml **egg whites** (about 6 eggs, at room temperature)

a pinch of **salt**

350g **caster sugar**

2 teaspoons **cornflour**

1 teaspoon **vanilla extract**

1 teaspoon **white wine vinegar**

### FOR THE PASSION FRUIT CURD

7 **passion fruit**

50g **butter**

70g **caster sugar**

1 **egg** + 2 **egg yolks**

50ml **Malibu**

300ml **double cream**, whipped

½ a **pineapple**, cut into chunks

1 **mango**, cut into chunks

**desiccated coconut**, toasted, to decorate

### VARIATIONS

Using the pavlova recipe above, try topping the whipped cream with these alternative ideas:

✿ Classic: 400g mixed berries (strawberries, raspberries, etc.)

✿ Drizzle custard over the cream and top with Rhubarb & Orange Compote (see page 40)

1. Heat the oven to 170°C/340°F/gas mark 3½ and line a baking sheet with baking parchment.

2. In a clean, dry bowl, whisk the egg whites with a pinch of salt until stiff peaks are formed.

3. Gradually add the sugar, 2 tablespoons at a time whisking after each addition, until the mixture is stiff and shiny. Whisk in the cornflour, then the vanilla and vinegar.

4. Turn the mixture out on to the prepared baking sheet and shape into a circle about 3–4cm deep. Place in the oven, then turn down the temperature to 120°C/250°F/gas mark ½ and cook for about 1 hour 30 minutes. Keep checking the pavlova to make sure it is not browning and adjust the oven accordingly. When it's hard on the outside but still soft inside, turn the oven off, open the door a little and leave to cool, still inside the oven.

5. To make the passion fruit curd, briefly blitz the pulp from 5 of the passion fruit in a blender, then sieve. Combine the juice with the pulp from the remaining fruit and place in a heatproof bowl with the butter, sugar, egg and egg yolks. Sit the bowl over a pan of gently simmering water and whisk the mixture until it thickens. Remove from the heat and set aside to cool.

6. Fold the Malibu into the whipped cream. Set the pavlova on a serving dish. Top with the Malibu whipped cream, pineapple and mango chunks, drizzle the passion fruit curd over the top and sprinkle with toasted coconut before serving.

or stewed blackberries or gooseberries.

✿ Chocolate sauce & raspberries.

✿ Stir rum into the whipped cream, then top with poached pears,

chocolate sauce, maple syrup and caramelized pecans.

✿ Fold toasted crushed cobnuts (or hazelnuts) into the meringue mix before baking.

# Our Favourite Cheesecake

SERVES 8–10 • PREPARATION TIME: 15 MINUTES • COOKING TIME: 1 HOUR • V

This is our favourite cheesecake … a very light one made with mascarpone, and baked in the oven until it has a slight wobble.

800g **mascarpone**

finely grated zest of 2 **lemons** and juice of 1

finely grated zest of 1 **orange**

seeds from 1 **vanilla pod**

4 **eggs**

350g **caster sugar**

1 tablespoon **crème fraîche**

1 tablespoon **double cream**

grated **nutmeg**

**dark chocolate**, to decorate

### FOR THE BASE

250g **dark chocolate digestive biscuits**

75g **butter**

75g **walnuts**, finely chopped

1. Line a 25cm springform cake tin with baking parchment.

2. First make the base. Either smash the digestives in a bag with a rolling pin or quickly blitz them in a food processor. Melt the butter in a pan and add the biscuits and chopped walnuts. Mix well and press into the base of the prepared tin. Refrigerate until needed.

3. Meanwhile, heat the oven to 150°C/300°F/ gas mark 2. Put the mascarpone into a large bowl. Add the citrus zests and lemon juice and the vanilla and mix well.

4. In a second bowl, whisk together the eggs and sugar until light. Gradually mix them into the mascarpone until you have a smooth cream.

5. Pour the mixture on to the cheesecake base and bake in the oven for 1 hour, or until just cooked, but still with a little wobble. Turn off the oven, but leave the cheesecake inside for 5 minutes. Then remove from the oven and leave to cool completely.

6. Mix the crème fraîche with the double cream and gently spread over the top of the cake. Finish with lots of grated nutmeg and dark chocolate.

**VARIATIONS**

❀ Try using ginger snap biscuits for the base instead of digestives, and substitute pecans for walnuts. If using these variations use lime juice instead of lemon in the cheese filling for a more tropical cheesecake. Serve with mango and pineapple.

**TIPS**

* Serve with a berry or Rhubarb & Orange Compote (see page 40).

# Blackberry & Apple Crumble

SERVES 8 • PREPARATION TIME: 20 MINUTES • COOKING TIME: 50 MINUTES • V Ⓥ

Lots of different fruits are used in crumbles and everyone has their favourite. This recipe is a well-known classic, the crumble topping unadulterated and simple. However, we have also given suggestions for other combinations of fruit and some variations on the toppings.

1.5kg **Braeburn apples**

400g **blackberries**

100g **soft brown sugar**

25g **butter**

a dash of **Calvados** (optional)

### FOR THE TOPPING

350g **plain flour**

a pinch of **salt**

250g **cold butter**, cut into small cubes

175g **caster sugar**

1. Heat the oven to 160°C/325°F/gas mark 3.

2. Peel and core the apples and cut them into 1–2cm chunks. Put them into a large ovenproof dish and add the berries and sugar. Dot the top with butter and drizzle over the Calvados (if using).

3. To make the topping, put the flour and salt into a food processor. Add the butter and process until the mix has gone past the breadcrumb stage and is starting to come up the sides of the mixer.

4. Tip the topping mixture into a large bowl, stir in the sugar and rub it all together with your fingertips. It is important that the crumble mixture is slightly lumpy, not dry like sawdust.

5. Sprinkle the crumble mixture over the fruit and bake in the oven for 40–50 minutes, or until golden brown on top.

### VARIATIONS

#### TOPPINGS

❀ Crushed amaretti biscuits, folded through the crumble mix – a favourite.

❀ Add a few porridge oats to the crumble mix.

❀ Add dark chocolate pieces and hazelnuts.

#### FRUIT COMBINATIONS

❀ Apples and blueberries.

❀ Pears with blackberries or blueberries.

❀ Rhubarb and strawberries.

❀ Rhubarb and blood oranges.

❀ Damsons, plums or greengages.

❀ Plums and blackberries.

### TIPS

* Best served hot, with custard or cream.

# LEON
## LABELS

LEON

LEON

LEON

LEON

LEON

LEON

LEON

# Banana & Baileys Parfait

SERVES 8 • PREPARATION TIME: 10 MINUTES • COOKING TIME: 4 HOURS •
FREEZING TIME: 6 HOURS • WF GF V ⓥ

The key to this heavenly ice cream is making sure that you boil your condensed milk early, as it takes 4 hours. It can be done the day, or even the week, before – just leave the tin (unopened) in your storecupboard and take it out when you're ready to make the parfait. This is a particularly good dessert to serve over the festive season.

2 x 400g tins of **condensed milk**
(or see Tips below)
100g **caster sugar**
100ml **water**
6 ripe **bananas**
250ml **Baileys**
440ml **double cream**

1. Put the unopened tins of milk into a large pan and cover with water. Bring to the boil, then reduce the heat and simmer for 4 hours, keeping the water topped up at all times. Allow to cool. This can be done days in advance.

2. Put the sugar and water into a pan and heat together until the sugar has dissolved, making a sugar syrup.

3. Now open your tins and put the toffeed milk, bananas, sugar syrup and Baileys into a food processor. Blitz until smooth, then transfer to a bowl.

4. Lightly whip the double cream until holding soft peaks and fold into the Baileys mixture.

5. Line a large terrine mould (or any container suitable for holding ice cream) with clingfilm and pour in the mixture. Freeze until firm (about 6 hours).

**TIPS**

* You can buy ready-made dulche de leche in a tin (called Nestlé Carnation cook with caramel), if you prefer.

* Keep an eye on the boiling tin of condensed milk. If the water in the pan dries out, the tin will explode and splatter goo all over your ceiling.

* Remember to take the parfait out of the freezer 15 minutes before serving to ensure the best texture.

* Best served drizzled with melted chocolate.

JONNIE, CHELTENHAM, 1974

LEON

This recipe was given to us by Jonnie who makes the Sauerkraut (see page 270). For someone who is now teaching macrobiotics and who once insisted on a wheat-free/dairy-free pudding, this indulgence comes as quite a surprise.

JANE

# Menu Ideas for Feeding Friends & Family

## BONFIRE NIGHT PARTY

**Corn Chowder** (see page 54)
**Stuffed Chillies** (see page 91)
**Simon's Potato Wedges**
    (see page 141)
**Squash, Corn & Bean Stew**
    (see page 189)
**Corn Fritters with Chunky**
    **Guacamole** (see page 208)

## WINTER SUNDAY LUNCH

**Addie May's Christmas**
    **Nut Loaf** (see page 166)
**Cauliflower Cheese**
    (see page 162)
**Leeks Vinaigrette** (see page 202)
**Turnips, Beetroot & Orange**
    (see page 204)
**Shredded Sprouts** (see page 219)
**Roast Potatoes** (see page 239)
**Joyce's Sticky Toffee Puddings**
    (see page 280)

## SOUTHERN ITALIAN LUNCH

**Orecchiette with Peas &**
    **Spinach** (see page 108)
**Puglian Bean Purée with**
    **Padrón Peppers**
    (see page 127)
**Aubergine Involtini**
    (see page 221)
**Fried Courgettes**
    (see page 255)
**Pickled Celery with Ricotta**
    (see page 274)

## NORTHERN ITALIAN NIGHT

**Squash Arancini**
    (see pages 114 & 21)
**Fonduta with Purple Sprouting**
    **Broccoli & Asparagus**
    (see page 35)
**Ribollita** (see page 56)
**Franco's Panzarotti**
    (see page 257)
**Polenta with Creamed Kale**
    (see page 234)

## SUMMER PICNIC

**Asparagus & Wild Garlic**
    **Frittata** (see page 32)
**Little Gem & Egg Salad with**
    **Aniseed Dressing**
    (see page 73)
**Salvatore's Panzanella**
    (see page 77)
**Leeks Vinaigrette**
    (see page 202)
**Potato Salad** (see page 242)
**Parsnip, Cashew & Coconut**
    **Cake** (see page 283)

## ASIAN SUPPER

**Mushroom Mapo Tofu**
    (see page 190)
**Henry's Basic Basmati Rice**
    (see page 195)
**Sweet Potato with Ginger,**
    **Garlic & Coriander**
    (see page 215)
**Aubergines with a Miso Glaze**
    (see page 220)
**Malaysian Tomato Salad**
    (see page 252)

## SRI LANKAN SUPPER

**Green Bean & Cashew Curry**
    (see page 172)
**Grated Beetroot Curry**
    (see page 178)
**Stir-fried Spiced Spring Greens**
    (see page 181)
**Dhal** (see page 185)
**Pineapple Curry** (see page 186)
**Sri Lankan Milk Rice**
    (see page 195)
**Henry's Basic Basmati Rice**
    (see page 195)

LEON.
EST. 2004
SUNSET
DRINKS

# Recipe Index

## WHEAT FREE

## GLUTEN FREE

## DAIRY FREE

## INDULGENCE

# Main Index

# Thank You

### FROM JANE

To Henry, for believing in me • Georgia, for the best pictures and being up for 'anything' • Anita, amazing designer, who is also up for 'anything' • Sue, who held it all together • Abi, so much more than a KP... but you do look fabulous in a pinny • The team on the photo shoots... the most disfunctional family possible, but who made the whole experience a complete joy with some unforgettable moments • My son David for being so great in a year when everything changed, and being a fun and tolerant travel companion when all he really wanted to do was to stay at home and watch the Simpsons • My Mum, brother John, Louise, Jacob and Laura (and Rusty) • My old crew at the FK... Sam, Ben, Jenny, Robin, Georgie, Pauline, Jonny, Adz and Rita XX • To Rose, Ruthie and Joyce... the best teachers and mentors • To all contributors especially; Christine and Dan who have opened my eyes (and doors) to La Bella Italia • Ben Bulger from the Magdalene Chapter in Exeter... nuff said • Mitch, Matt, Tim and all the boys from the truffle trip and The Seahorse in Dartmouth • All our friends in Italy who have been unwittingly the greatest inspiration ... Salvatore, Pietro Zito, Katarina and Santina (Caprai and Antonelli wines) • Addie May... best Nut loaf ever! • Vicky from Whiteley's Farm in the Rhubarb Triangle • Jonnie, (Sarah and Leila Rose) for teaching us about the dark fermentation arts • Henry's mum, Jossy • Simon from the Crabshell with Sonia, Louis, Freya and Millie (very good Orecchiette makers) • Bob Granleese and Jacq Burns • Kate Dahill... great support and contributor on the shoots (bit on the side!) • Franco and Ann in Abergavenny • Oisin Rogers #fridge buffet • Katie's mum, Pat • Leah and her Bramble Café • All the Sisters of Doom #SOD... you know who you are? • Lara , Sasha and all at Coombe Farm Studios for bringing some sun into the grey dark November days of the last shoot • Martin Orbach and Juliette... for all the support over the last few years • Mandy... for listening to my gin rants • Bill Gunn and Ross Mc Killop... for mutual taro hatred and love of palusami • Sybella, Alison and all at Conran Octopus.

### FROM HENRY

John for transforming the Leon menu as this book was being written • Our FD Matt for not just holding the fort but building a few more turrets • Giles for another great recipe and for turning round people's perceptions of school food • Beth my great ally in the battle against entropy • Glenn, Justin, Nickie and Alan for making the Leon restaurants such lovely places to be • Top, Tom, James and Danny for turning dreams into reality • Steve, Agnieszka and Christina for making it all add up • Be, property intern, the lady with the most glamorous job title in business, thank you for spirit and dedication • Bruno Loubet for getting me started and inspiring me every time we meet • Quentin Letts, who taught me never to use the word 'meal' • Megan and Caina, oh, the beauty! • Jane Gerber for telling so many wonderful stories • Anita and Georgia, what a tremendous pleasure it has been to have worked with you • Sybella, our editor, eternally cool and cheering • Alison for picking up the baton with such enthusiasm • Fiona, we miss you already • Mum and Dad, for never suggesting for a moment that what we were doing was madness.

### FROM ANITA & GEORGIA

Sue, oh Sue, wonderful assistant to Georgia • Abi for excellent design assistance, being the token teenager and modelling in the dressing gown, pinny and cape • Shumei Organic Farm and the Yatesbury allotments for allowing us to photograph their lovely veg • Le Creuset for pots and pans • Bryony, Maddy and Gemma • Mattma, Maddie and Cy • Stef, Daisy and Poppy • Henry and Jane, first class skippers, especially in a row boat • A big thanks for all our sense of humours. She made me say that.

# The Leon Team

Abdelhadi Fekier
Adebusola Ogunsanya
Adriana Oliviero
Agata Cyminska Thomas
Agnieszka Chmieliauskas
Agnieszka Jablonska
Aimi Walker
Alan Mcniven
Aleksandra Kralewska
Alessio Greco
Alessio Simonetta
Alexander Ferguson
Algirdas Visockis
Alicja Pawlitko
Amita Shrestha
Anderson Gomcalves
Andrea Papalini
Andres Gruber
Andrius Venclovas
Anna Anuscenko
Anna Miller
Anna Sterczala
Annie Grant
Antonio Fernandes
Anu Rego
Arturas Marma
Asta Gostautaite
Barbora Guobyte
Ben Iredale
Bernardo Aragao
Beth Emmens
Beverley Morgan
Bilan Ahmed
Blandine Vinard
Bozena Bobowska
Caina Bertussi Rotta
Carl Pattrick
Carlos Da Cruz Moreira
Carlos Martinez Munecas
Cayelan Mendoza
Cecilia Hoijertz
Cerita Woolcock
Charles Casey
Charles Matthews
Charlotte Dixon
Christopher Finney
Christopher Ford
Ciara Smith
Claire Didier
Clara Bleda Megias

Clare Cole
Claudia Morais Caldeir
Claudinei Da Silva
Cleiton Francisco Da Silva
Cristina Bertani
Daniel Pittman
Danny de Ruiter
Daria Zvab
Dario Polo
Davide Dabala
Denzso Zrinszki
Dominic Sherington
Donatas Bajorunas
Edvinas Marma
Egle Rimaite
Egle Rinkselyte
Egle Semetaite
Eimear White
Eszter Hajnal
Evijs Ozols
Ewan Milne
Fabio Rodrigues
Ferenc Csillag
Francesca Carubia
Frederico Balbi Amatto
Fumi Opeyemi
Gabor Salai
Gil Rubin
Giovanni Muoio
Glenn Edwards
Guenzit Tanoh
Guilherme Coelho
Gytis Sirvinskas
Harris Nazinou
Hayley Osborne
Heather Wallis
Henry Dimbleby
Holly Clare
Ineta Bliudziute
Irene Frances Argente
Istvan Szep
Izatoj Chodzamkulova
Jacob Charlton
James Charnock
James French
Jaroslaw Bodzioch
Jenna Brehme
Jirina Kralova
John Corrigan
John Vincent

Jorge Casadejus Sevilla
Jose Rodriguez Rozo
Joshua Martin
Juan Matienzo
Julian Gomes
Jurgita Sirvinskiene
Justas Pokvytis
Justin Ovenden
Justina Ciuksyte
Kadija Begum
Kalina Sikorska
Karolina Driessen
Katre Kurosu
Kayleigh Goodger
Kimberley Frost
Kristel Maley
Kristen Rego
Kristina Dabkeviciene
Lacey Lawson
Laia Baron Selles
Laszlo Moricz
Laura Maniura
Laura Oakley
Lauren Roberts
Leandro Da Silva
Liliya Georgieva
Louis Sock
Louisa Hessmert
Lucy Buckingham
Lukas Drotar
Lukasz Fiedler
Lukasz Kubiak
Lysette Cook
Maciej Marek
Maija Bika
Maja Bodekaer Black
Malgorzata Herda
Manuela Crivellari
Marc-Alexis Constance
Marco Berardi
Maria Capuano
Maria Paton Martinez
Mariana Kastrati
Marta Diaz Gutierrez
Martyn Trigg
Matthew Alp
Matthew Fogg
Matthew Jones
Matthias Abdel-Haiat
Meena Shinwari

Megan Bailey-Ward
Megan Blyth
Mercy Okereke
Meritxell Gabarra
Michaela Boor
Michaela O'Neill
Micheline Essomba
Miguel Tavares
Mindaugas Sirvinskas
Mirela Hapsa
Monika Kwiatkowska
Mourad Moukhlis
Natalia Farnaus
Navina Senivassen
Nichola Norton
Nickie Bartsch
Nicola Kibble
Nicoleta Vitelaru
Nikki Gardham
Nilton Caboco
Nina Amaniampong
Nina Duffekova
Nina Jaworska
Nora Goboly
Nora Szosznyak
Olga Chwilowicz
Olivia Tweedale
Olivier Aka-Kadjo
Olumide Otusajo
Oscar Otero
Osiur Khan
Pablo Garcia Del Olmo
Patricia Boronat
Patricia Ferreira Martins
Paulo Rodrigues
Pedro Barchin
Pedro Candida
Philippe Mesquita
Rabbani Mahbuby
Rachael Gough
Radoslaw Zemsta
Rasa Raskeviciute
Reda el Guebli
Remigijus Chmieliauskas
Richard Clifford
Roberta Rimkute
Robin Guiomar
Rory Mcloughlin
Rute Coelho Da Rocha
Salvatore Scarpa

Salvija Dargyte
Samuel Usero Valencia
Samuele Raiano
Sandra Navarro
Sara Antonelli
Sara Hidalgo
Sebastian Ruiz
Sebestyen Zalay
Shaun Stanley
Simona Andreoni
Simona Cijunskyte
Simona Vysniauskaite
Sini Mulari
Solomon Henry
Stephen Bage
Stephen Oakley
Suzanna Hurst
Talita Heshiimu
Thiago Turibio Da Silva
Thomas Davies
Thomas Green
Thomas Hill-Caluori
Thomas Malley
Tia Marks
Tom Bailey
Tran Nguyen Hoang
Trianee Bluey
Vadim Ivanov
Vasilica Cirican
Viktoria Raj
Vydmante Kalvynaite
Wendy Xiaowen Zhang
Georgiou
Yaakoeb Daoudi
Yok Chung
Zoe Masson
Zoheir Benalia

First published in 2014 by Conran Octopus Limited, a part of Octopus Publishing Group, Endeavour House, 189 Shaftesbury Avenue, London WC2H 8JY
www.octopusbooks.co.uk

An Hachette UK Company
www.hachette.co.uk

British Library Cataloguing-in-Publication Data. A catalogue record for this book is available from the British Library.

Publisher: Alison Starling
Senior Editor: Sybella Stephens
Art Direction, Styling & Design: Anita Mangan
Art Director (for Conran Octopus): Jonathan Christie
Design Assistant: Abigail Read
Photography: Georgia Glynn Smith
Senior Production Manager: Katherine Hockley

ISBN 978 1 84091 610 2
Printed in China

A note from the authors…
We have endeavoured to be as accurate as possible in all the preparation and cooking times listing in the recipes in this book. However they are an estimate based on our own timings during recipe testing, and should be taken as a guide only, not as the literal truth. Nutrition advice is not absolute. If you feel you require consultation with a nutritionist, consult your GP for a recommendation.

Not all cheese is vegetarian – check the label or ask your cheesemonger if you are unsure.

Picture credits
**Alamy** Florilegius 17 below left and right.
**Bridgeman Art Library** The Stapleton Collection 16 above right, 17 above, 283.
**RHS Images** RHS, Lindley Library 16 below right, 17 below centre, 146, 227, 252.
**Shutterstock** Madlen 49 right; Sandra Zuerlein 49 left.
**Garry and Jaquine Oliver-Purchase** 186

QUEEN OF SAINT MARTHE